I0558259

READER BONUS!

Dear Reader,

As a thank you for your support, Action Takers Publishing would like to offer you a special reader bonus: a free download of our course, How to Write, Publish, Market & Monetize Your Book the Fast, Fun & Easy Way." This comprehensive course is designed to provide you with the tools and knowledge you need to bring your book to life and turn it into a successful venture.

The course typically **retails for $499,** but as a valued reader, you can access it for free. To claim your free download, simply follow this link <u>ActionTakersPublishing.com/ workshops</u> - use the discount code "coursefree" to get a 100% discount and start writing your book today.

If we are still giving away this course by the time you're reading this book, head straight over to your computer and start the course now. It's absolutely free.

READER BONUS!

<u>ActionTakersPublishing.com/workshops</u>
discount code "coursefree"

WOMEN

— WITH —

HEALING

GIFTS

Breaking Barriers and Changing the World

Email: lynda@actiontakerspublishing.com

Website: www.actiontakerspublishing.com

ISBN # (paperback) 978-1-956665-30-7

ISBN # (Kindle) 978-1-956665-31-4

Published by Action Takers Publishing™

Dedications

I dedicate this to all the women who don't buy into the false truths they are told they should settle for. From false diagnosis to body shaming, ageism or bullying in the workplace, family, or spousal relationships. You have a powerful resource that is your birthright, You are woman. Your birthright is your healing gift.

~Lorrel Elian

To healing the Past, Present and Future here now. Dedication of my chapter goes to Nico'l Elisa and Noah Bear. Love is BElonging.

~ChristianeAnna Rodriguez

Words alone cannot express how thankful I am to you. You have been my source of strength, inspiration, and guidance. You taught me to be unique, determined, and to always persevere. You will always be in my heart, Nanny.

~Dina Legland

This chapter is dedicated to my Creator, my loving father and mother and to the countless souls I have encountered in my journey of life so far - each one has had a lasting impact on my story and has added so much value to the tapestry of my life. It is also dedicated to you, the reader. There is a reason this book is in your hands and I pray you receive what you need from the words in this book. May you know joy in your heart.

~Dina Sabnani

Sincere thank you to my children, Kerri Pacheco and David Cerra, for bearing witness to my choices in life and loving me through the process. You have been there for me even before conception. I knew who you were and you, in turn, now know me.

~Gail Kraft

I dedicate this book to all the people in my life who have supported, influenced, and aided me in the care of people in my life. My in-laws and my family in the care of my husband Milton for twenty years. To my family and assistance in the care of my father. And, to all the nurses, doctors, and ancillary help in the hospitals in caring for very ill patients in my efforts to offer comfort and hope during their journey to wellness or end of life. Thank you all from the bottom of my heart.

~Janet Ward

This work is dedicated to all of the women who have held enough courage in their hearts to do things differently than how the world has been telling them they should.

~Lauren Best

To God, thank you for this human experience. I am in deep gratitude for my life. To my Ancestors, thank you for always nudging me to do better, and be better than what you could have done.

~Melissa Renee Yannitell

This chapter is dedicated to my mom. Thank you for all the listening and spacious presence you have given me that has allowed me to find and follow my own paths.

~Michel Spruance

This is for my baby brother, Nizam, the bravest boy I know. Some people don't believe in heroes, but they haven't met my brother. It's been an honor growing up with you. Ready to face whatever life sends, joy and laughter or tears and strife, holding hands tightly as we dance through life…

~Nasirra R Ahamed

I dedicate this to my mom. She always inspired me to be my best self and I am thankful for her guidance throughout my life. She will always have a special place in my heart. I love you Mom!

~Sally Green

My chapter is dedicated to YHWH, for bestowing my healing gifts to me, my kids for giving me a purpose greater than myself, and my clients for allowing me to share my talents with them.

~Shanna Lee Moore

I dedicate this book to my amazing girls, Avery Jewel and Sophia Madison, who inspire me to be the best Mom I can be every day because you deserve nothing but the very best. I adore everything about the two of you and love you with all my heart and soul! I also dedicate this book to my Dad, Ronnie Roper, I am me because there was you. Thank you for being exactly the Dad I needed so I can be the Mom I am; I stand on your shoulders and will always look up to you for wisdom.

~Tiffiny Roper

To everyone I have ever had the privilege to do a session for. It has been an honor to see your trust in God and desire for miracles to unfold, to be your Possibility Coach™, and to share in the sacredness of life. May you continue to be blessed daily!

~Victoria Rader, Ph.D.

Table of Contents

Introduction

In a world where healing takes on countless forms, there exists an extraordinary group of women who possess innate gifts and talents that transcend boundaries. They are the healers, the visionaries, the trailblazers—the ones who are courageously reshaping the world with their unique abilities. In this collaborative book, "Women with Healing Gifts: Breaking Barriers and Changing the World," we embark on a transformative journey through the remarkable stories of 22 extraordinary women, each bringing their own extraordinary healing gifts to the forefront.

This book celebrates the power of women who have harnessed their healing abilities to challenge societal norms, defy expectations, and inspire change. From traditional practices to innovative modalities, these women have fearlessly embraced their calling, devoting their lives to bringing healing to individuals, communities, and the world at large. They have shattered barriers and transcended limitations, illuminating a path for others to follow.

As you immerse yourself in the narratives of these women, you will be moved by their strength, resilience, and unwavering dedication to their respective paths. Each chapter uncovers the personal journeys, triumphs, and challenges of these remarkable individuals, inviting you to reflect on your own relationship with healing and empowerment. Through their stories, you will find inspiration, encouragement, and a profound sense of possibility.

"Women with Healing Gifts: Breaking Barriers and Changing the World" is not only a tribute to the transformative power of women but also a collective call to action. It urges us to recognize and honor the innate healing abilities that reside within each of us, irrespective of gender. It encourages us to embrace our unique gifts and use them to create a more harmonious and compassionate world.

May this book serve as a catalyst for change, a beacon of hope, and a reminder that healing knows no bounds. Let the stories within these pages kindle a fire within you, empowering you to step into your own healing journey and play a part in the collective transformation we all long for.

Welcome to the empowering world of "Women with Healing Gifts: Breaking Barriers and Changing the World."

CHAPTER 1

How I Discovered My Healer's Gift
and Mastered My Life

by Lorrel Elian

I discovered my healing gift through health challenges that almost cost me my life. At some point in your life, you have a moment when you ask the question, What's it all about?

Are you that Girl?

Are you at a crossroads, questioning? Going through a divorce, experienced the death of a loved one, or you're dealing with a critical health challenge. I discovered a place where most women arrive after an internal struggle. They bravely continue to maneuver through their stress and mundane daily duties while they bury, or ignore, the trauma that haunts them. For many, if they don't find a solution, it can **kill them**.

At the very least, the stress impacts the quality of their relationships, even how much money they make. It prematurely ages them, and definitely affects their health. I call this very real occurrence, the Body Mind Intersection. When an accumulation of trauma, disguised as emotional baggage, finally meets the boiling point, and you can no longer ignore the pain that physically, emotionally and psychologically drains you. You can no longer avoid, deny or continue to stuff down all the emotions you've been **managing** for way too long. If you're that woman, this is for you. I get you, I know how your heart works. I understand how you suffer because you're me. You suspect there is more to life than what you're living, but don't know how to change it or get out from under it.

Do you struggle with the pressure of the tiring daily routine of: Get up, go to work, get everyone else ready first? Feel trapped in a life, or a body that you feel powerless in? Maybe there's guilt or shame for wanting precious alone time to recuperate from all the hats you wear. If you're a mom, you suffer even more. You give so much to everyone all day long, and at the end of the day, who's there for you? The body mind intersection is where your reality and desires collide.

You've been carrying your burdens for so long. Being the trooper you are, you continue to get up every day, put on your lipstick, roll up your sleeves, and dig in with a willingness to make things work. You tell yourself, maybe today will be the day it'll change. Have you lost your confidence, sense of self-worth, or enthusiasm for life? Do you feel like you've lost your identity? You know there's more than what you've been living. You've suffered emotional and/or physical pain and work to convince yourself that you've dealt with the past. You've tried everything to let go and move forward, and still it haunts you.

Girlfriend, it's time to release the emotional burdens you've been carrying for way too long. It prematurely ages you and makes you sick. I've dedicated my life to finding the answers to my own painful journey. I'm proof. You're never too old, too sick or out of shape to make a comeback. Turn your mess into your message and discover the truth of who you are meant to be.

My spirit was deeply buried in my body, literally! A lifetime of being told who and what I was supposed to be, how I was to act and feel, that I lost myself. I had such low self-esteem I didn't identify trauma as the cause of my pain. I always knew I was different, today I understand why.

My healing journey was more than on this physical plane. As I reclaimed my life, and healed my body, I discovered my healing powers.

My wish for you is to reclaim your life and write your own heroine's journey. You're not meant to suffer. Your struggle is part of your life's mystery, you're meant to use it for empowerment.

Discover the truth of who you are, and why you're here. The answers you seek are already in you, I promise. Before you were born, the stars aligned to create you. You were born out of light; your body is made of stardust. You are a child of the universe, you're here to share your gifts.

Each of us has a human struggle. That's how we discover the truth of who we are.

Turning My Mess Into My Message

I'll always remember that day I heard the voice. The inside view of my body was up on a large screen in a diagnostic lab. While I lay most uncomfortably, hooked up by cables to the machine.

My internal organs were the focus for the medical technicians, who were busy adjusting dials and probes and reading the data. The darkened room was cold and industrial, unfeeling.

It reminded me of watching a bad movie. I was screaming inside and no one even knew I was there. I was just a body, an object.

I focused on being disconnected from my body, and from what was going on around me.

A habit I practiced too often. This was another procedure, on a long list of procedures and surgeries that I hoped would finally give doctors the answers they needed to explain the mysterious pain in my body. This day, the scene was the most impersonal. They worked on their instruments and machines around me, and in me. The probe inserted in my body left me feeling powerless and stripped of any dignity. As thoughts whirled in my head, wondering when they would be done, a very clear and distinct, masculine voice came over the loudspeaker in my head. **Lady, get your shit together.**

It was not unusual to have conversations going on in my head. This time it was different, it was not a voice I recognized. Clear, abrupt, and almost sarcastic, the voice demanded that I pay attention. As I headed to my car, the echo of the voice played over in my head, "Lady, get your shit together." I sat in my car for a while to gather my thoughts before heading back into the busy traffic. I felt numb, what was I to do? So many tests and procedures without answers. Something had to change. Maybe **I** had to change? I wanted out of the powerless feeling in my life, and my body. I felt like I had worked so hard to be happy and healthy, but this pattern of illness and often unidentifiable pain followed me.

Repeating Life Patterns

Ten years earlier, a similar situation had played out. A week after exchanging vows with my beloved, I received a letter from my doctor. I had a full physical a few weeks before the wedding. Blood work revealed negative markers that a biopsy later confirmed. I was in stage three of uterine cancer and booked for emergency surgery. Two weeks after the surgery, I called the surgeon's office for the results. I had already suspected that if they had something urgent to tell me, they would have called. "Sometimes these things just leave," the nurse said over the phone, "We don't fully understand why." I started smiling. The results of the surgery were negative. I was awake during the biopsy while the surgeon described what he was seeing.

The nurse responded with, "The cancer left; it was just gone. Sometimes it just does that; we can't explain it."

Really, could it be that simple? There had to be more to it than that. It didn't just go away.

I had gotten really busy working with my body and my mind before that surgery date.

My herbalist friend was actually excited as she explained, "this is easier to get rid of than arthritis. You've got this!"

I had two little girls to raise. If I weren't there, what would happen to them? I knew it wasn't my time to leave.

Sometimes when you're given a gift, you don't see the true value. I have personally known women who didn't survive the same diagnosis. I knew what had happened was a big deal, and in that moment, I felt pretty powerful.

Then, as often happens, I went on with my life and the memory of my victory over cancer faded. Healthier habits in my lifestyle and stress slipped back in.

Life got busy raising kids, having a career, doing all the daily tasks that people *think* they're supposed to do. Be a good wife, an awesome mom. Have a great house, drive a nice car.

"Shop, eat steak and chase a ball around a green" (as one of my spiritual teachers put it).

Until this day. I was keeping up with life and completely exhausted from it. I had been ignoring the loud messages my body had been sending. Mentally & emotionally, I was drained from keeping up with all the hats I wore. This career was the one I had dreamed of for so long.

Sadly, I thought I would love it more.

I was a realtor in a booming market. I often worked with people who were making their first substantial purchase. The stress for many clients was often more than they knew how to manage. I was on the receiving end of many emotional moments. I had been excited to be a realtor, I thought it would be my dream job. I wanted to help people. Because of the crazy housing boom, I was often treated like the enemy. I wasn't emotionally equipped to be in this environment. A trap so many people fall into, staying in toxic environments for money because they think they don't have any other choice.

My body was screaming at me to pay attention.

The Inner Journey

There were so many red flags. I was clinically depressed, yet I would smile like everything was wonderful. I was in denial of having stress that was causing my world, and body to be on the verge of collapse. On the outside, everything looked pretty great. The house, the car, the kids, the great husband. I felt so guilty! I had everything, yet I was so empty. I felt so fake. I sat in my car thinking about the voice's message, and the years of demanding work. The sacrifices to build all we had. My husband worked overseas, the money was amazing, but he was away for months at a time. It was all supposed to be worth it. Worth what?

My physical condition had completely gone south. I stuffed my emotions down with food. The mask I wore for the outside world was to smile and pretend like everything was perfect. I was a time bomb. I cried at the drop of a dime. I woke up tired, even if I slept.

I had had fourteen surgeries since I was twenty-three. Now they were talking about another. Almost every day I had pain, even as a kid.

Years later, I discovered that this dis-ease has many names. It's the psychosomatic symptom that occurs physically when we emotionally carry trauma. It's the silent killer of dreams. I didn't associate what was happening as trauma related. It's a blind spot in our awareness. We can't see it, but others do. It's insidious in the way it integrates into your life through your personality, your emotions and habits. I'm too busy, I don't have time, I'm sick and tired. It's active in your life right now, and you don't see it. Then, I remembered the gift. If I was able to obliterate cancer from my life, why not this?

Emotional Breakthrough

No one could have prepared me for the journey ahead. I wouldn't have believed them. Discovering what was at the root of all my pain was not a short journey. Reconciling the dis-ease and dysfunction in my life was where the relief came from.

When I look back, I see how I'd always been divinely guided, although I was totally unconscious to the efforts of the universe trying to wake me up.

I struggled in my relationship with siblings, and I often found myself alone. I didn't fit in most places, even in my family. The feeling of being on the outside, looking in was my norm.

So I filled the void with imagination and creativity. I loved reading about people's struggles and how they overcame adversity. The weird, the outlandish, even alien, was intriguing to me. I dreamed of faraway places. Egypt, Atlantis and mystical temples. I would fly through starry galaxies when I closed my eyes at night. My childhood passed quickly as I wished it away, hoping to find magical cities beyond the uneventful neighborhood I lived in.

As I evaluated my alternative options for healing, I opened my imagination again.

I was fortunate to have had teachers from ancient lineages.

They opened my mind to looking at my life, my body in a new light. I started to see how life was not random. I travelled to sacred temples and studied mystical arts and healing. I became a student of ancient cultures and sacred geometry. I learned from Masters of Yoga, feng shui, numerology, Sanskrit. The universe responded in a magical way.

I was fascinated how texts written thousands of years before could guide me. Discovering the body-mind connection was my big breakthrough. It led me to classical hatha yoga. I craved how good it felt to be in my body! I'd lived my whole life without experiencing this. I moved into deeper studies and completed many certifications.

I became a master of reading form and energy. I travelled the world, reading faces, doing energy clearing and workshops. The forgotten clairsentient gifts I had shut down as a child, started returning. This time, with awareness and maturity, I started to cultivate them.

As my health returned, my body and life started looking different too.

Sometime after that triggering day in the diagnostic lab, my surgeon phoned. He wondered how I was and if there was anything he could do for me. It was very grim the last time I saw him.

His kindness moved me. I reflected on how the most uncomfortable time in my life forced me to find my healer within. It took the pain in my body to wake up.

I became intensely aware of how to best nourish my brain and body. Discovering how many of the issues related to the pain I was experiencing came from the fear and trauma I had deeply buried.

I had become conscious of my thoughts, my words and the way I treated my body. I learned how thoughts become your body's messaging system, and how that forms the shape your body becomes. I became a therapist, an expert in my field of body-mind communication. The healthier I became physically, the stronger I was emotionally. Oppressive relationships that were challenging, even painful, healed or went away. The tears had long since dried as I became filled with purpose. All areas of my life were affected by my newfound resilience.

I had finally found that thing I was searching for. I had found what gave me purpose. This is my life's work.

You Can Change Your DNA

I was fifty, the year I completed my first teacher certifications in yoga and psychosomatics. I created courses for people to heal their lives and body. I loved teaching yoga using psychosomatic sequencing. I created Blended Body Sculpting and Somatic Face Therapy. Processes that re-program you at a cellular level and reverse ageing while you're discovering your inner world, your intuition. That was more than a comeback year. I really had started to live. I celebrated with a special birthday party. I spent more on my birthday cake than I had on my wedding cake! The results show in the photos I have from then. I looked and felt like I was twenty years younger.

On a cellular level, I am not the same person. I no longer look like my biological family, nor do I have their dis - eases or health issues.

When I see the adults that my grown children have become, they prove to me that the work I've done on myself has also impacted their quality of life.

How You Do One Thing Affects All Things

How you feel about what's happened to you affect the way you show up in life. Your thoughts shape you, your emotions shape you. Every thought has an emotion behind it. Your brain holds onto all of it.

Over a decade of reading faces and working with bodies, as a therapist and a teacher, I have learned that this is true. What you think, what you hear, the words you speak, who you spend time with, what you eat and even where you eat, will affect you and shape you. I facilitated healing retreats that were spiritual and self-empowering for over a decade. I learned so much from observing others in their healing process.

Your brain is a super computer connected to a 3D printer. Your thoughts are processed by the motherboard and feelings give energy to the emotions that shape your body and your life. The result is why you, and your life look the way they do.

Look deeper inside yourself to discover the underlying cause of what is making you feel the way you do. This means being honest with yourself in a way you may not have done before. Your thoughts, your environment and reactions play a larger role in your health and quality of life than most people accept.

You will only get as far as you know, that's why you must reach out in a new direction for knowledge. Nothing changes till you change.

Your life is the greatest body of work you'll complete in this lifetime. Make it a Masterpiece.

Lorrel Elian

Lorrel Elian is a three-time international best-selling author, mentor, speaker, and has been helping women discover their inner and outer beauty for over thirty years.

She's an expert on generational trauma and teaches life path healing through numerology and birth codes.

For over two decades she's facilitated workshops, training and healing retreats. Lorrel has been internationally certified as a Master face reader, Psychosomatic Teacher, Hatha yoga teacher.

Lorrel is the creator of Sacred Sound Therapy, Somatic Face Therapy, and Life Mastery Activation. Living a chemical free lifestyle and being a certified organic landowner has played a major role in how she responds to the world around her. Lorrel has dedicated her life to spirituality, quantum healing and teaching mind-body practices. She's passionate about living consciously by respecting mother earth. She lives in the heart of Canada on the prairies with her husband, Larry and her fur babies.

Her side passions are:

- time at the beach & paddle boarding

- practicing & teaching yoga

- teaching crystal singing bowls

- X-country Skiing on their organic farmland shared with deer, moose & beaver

- creating workshops in the sacred arts

Lorrel and Larry are building their second house that incorporates feng shui principles and sacred geometry. Together they are enthusiastic plant based foodies and organic landowners passionate about growing their own food and living a clean life: body, mind, and soul.

Connect with Lorrel at https://www.lorrelelian.com

CHAPTER 2

Fear Breathed Life Into Me

by Lynda Sunshine West

While fear can be scary, it can also be very liberating. In 2015, at the age of 51, I decided to embark on a journey of breaking through one fear a day for an entire year. I had no idea when I made that decision what my life would look like eight years later.

> *"You'll never know who you won't meet until you step outside of your comfort zone."* ~Lynda Sunshine West

Why is it that we have fear in the first place? Yeah, I get it, when we were living in caves and we needed to fight off lions and tigers and bears, oh my, it was our protection mechanism. But why do we still experience fear today? And why is it that we allow our fears to stop us from living our lives? And how can we use our fears to fuel us forward instead of holding us back? These questions and more will be answered in this chapter that you are about to read, from my perspective as a human being who broke through one fear every single day, 365 days in a row. I am not a doctor or a scientist or a researcher. I am simply a woman who took matters into my own hands and decided that fear was no longer going to control my life.

I grew up in a very volatile, abusive alcoholic household and ran away when I was five years old. I was gone for a week. What happened during that week was something that would shape the next 46 years of my life. You see, nobody came to get me. I was at the neighbor's house and was safe, but what I really wanted was to be loved and feel included. I believe my mom knew where I was and that I was safe (she's since passed on and I can't ask her), and that she was allowing me to "exercise my independence" even at that young age. She knew the neighbor and knew that the neighbor would take good care of me. However, as a 5-year-old child, I didn't see it that way. How I saw it was that nobody came to get me, and it must be because they don't love me and don't want me around.

One week after having a great time at my friend's house playing Barbie's and dress up, my mom called the neighbor and said, "Lynda has been gone long enough. You can send her home now." So I came home with my tail between my legs, riddled with fears, and became a people pleaser.

For those who don't know what a people pleaser is (hopefully you don't know what it is), it is somebody who, according to WebMD.com, "is typically someone everyone considers helpful and kind. When you need help with a project or someone to help you study for an exam, they're more than willing to step up. If you recognize yourself in the above description, you may be a people pleaser." While WebMD.com's description sounds harmless, being a people pleaser can create havoc and be a detriment.

One of the things I realized while I was breaking through one fear a day for an entire year is that the majority of my life was spent putting everybody else first and I had a strong desire for people to just like me. As a matter of fact, I was scared to say anything opposite from people because I had this tremendous fear that if I didn't agree with them that they wouldn't like me. I used to pride myself and call myself a chameleon. I could get along with anybody. The reality is that I was too scared for anybody to not like me, so I would just get along to make everything smooth and calm.

This behavior actually started in my household because of my dad's volatility. When he was at home, we walked on eggshells. I learned a behavior to be quiet and not voice my own opinions. I carried that behavior around with me until I was 51 years old, the year I hired a life coach who helped me to discover who I truly am and to step up as that person. At first, it was scary to state my own opinion because, again, that fear of going against other people was a strong fear because I just wanted everybody to like me.

What I came to realize while working with my life coach is that it's impossible to please everybody and that my opinions and voice do matter. She took me down this path of learning that it's necessary for me to share my thoughts and opinions because this is who I really am. When we show up as ourselves in all of our glory, we have tremendous power. When walking through life full of fear, it's impossible to be glorious and to have a greater impact on the planet.

In the process of breaking through one fear every day for a year, I created my own process that made breaking through fears easier and easier every day. By having a system in place, it made the fears not so scary. Because of that journey of breaking through fears every day, fear no longer stops me from living my life. As a matter of fact, I have a new mantra and that is to "Do It BECAUSE You're Scared."

One of the things I love about being a human being is that we have choice, freedom of choice. Sometimes our choices lead to terrible results, amazing results, and other times our choices lead to mediocre results. I believe one of the reasons people are scared of trying new things is because they are unsure what results they will receive. Society has gotten us to the place where it wants us to be perfect in more ways than possible. This perfection syndrome leads to fear.

When I was breaking through those fears, I started looking at the common theme behind the fears. I had a startling realization that the vast majority of my fears were centered around the fear of judgment. I had been scared of judgment since I was five years old. They say that we are a product of our environment. Growing up in a judgmental environment created a judgmental young lady who was afraid of judgment. It's kind of this cyclical situation where I was judgmental and, therefore, I was scared of judgment. Let me break this down.

Oftentimes in life when something bothers us about somebody, it's really something that bothers us about ourselves. I've heard this called the mirror effect, but don't know much about it. I just know that I had an epiphany one day about how I was judging others but, in reality, I was my own worst enemy because I was extremely judgmental against myself. Not only was I judgmental of other people, but I was judgmental of myself and this created within me a mean streak of being judgmental of others.

As I continued down my personal development journey, I started noticing that I became less and less judgmental of myself. The task I was focused on at that time was to discover my own brilliance and to use it in my life and business. About three years into my journey, I was attending an event and I saw this woman who was dressed impeccably, and she looked incredible. As I looked at her from across the room, I noticed something different, about me. I didn't judge her. (Well, maybe a little bit of judgment, but a different kind of judgment.) I judged her from a place of love and a place where as I looked at her I noticed how beautiful she was and decided to walk over to her and tell her. In the past, I never would have done that because I never would have seen how beautiful she was. I would have just judged her for thinking that she thinks she's better than everybody there. That's the way I was.

Fortunately, as human beings, we get to make decisions to do something different. And I'm glad I did. When I was breaking through those fears, so many different emotions showed up on a daily basis. I had an opportunity to shift the way I think. Since I realized that the fear of judgment was a big fear of mine, I was able to work on that one fear for the rest of the year.

There are a few fears that stand out to me that I remember as if they were yesterday. One of those was to "talk to a stranger in a Starbucks." Why was this such a scary thing for me? The fear of judgment. "What if I say something stupid?" "What if I look a weird way?" "What if he thinks I'm a weirdo?" "What if I don't know what to say?" All of these "what if" questions were creating fear within me. One of the things I learned to do was to ask myself questions, or, what I like to call "switch it." For example, when I say, "What if I say something stupid?," I would say to myself the words "flip it. What if I say something smart?" This one small act of flipping my words to something positive started to create a wave of possibility and positivity in my life. I had no idea when I started flipping my language around what would happen.

By simply flipping my language, my fears would subside. They would never fully disappear, but they would lessen. The more I started flipping my language, the more I recognized I needed to flip my language. It's kind of interesting how things like that go hand in hand. The more I flipped my language, the more positive I became. It's through the process of having awareness of what's going on around us that we can effect change. Until we have awareness, change is rare.

What would your life be like if you experienced less fear? What types of things would you do? How would you live your life? Would you allow what you're doing now to continue? Only you can answer these questions.

I came up with a new motto to do it BECAUSE you're scared because I realized something about fear. The vast majority of time when we break through fears, the results that we get are greater than we ever imagined they might be or we may be proud of ourselves for having broken through that fear. If this is the case, why do we prevent ourselves from being proud or getting greater results than we ever imagined? Had I not broken through those fears every day for a year, I have no idea what my life would be like today. Every single thing in my life today is different than it was in 2014 as a result of my breaking through those fears. As I stand here today, I love myself, I love my life, I love who I have become, I love the things I have done in life, I love the trajectory of my life. By breaking through those fears, life was breathed into me. Prior to that, I had spent my life in a cloud like a zombie just living day-to-day. I had no purpose or passion. I was just here.

I've heard this saying of feel the fear and do it anyway. To me, that's a very disempowering statement. I prefer to flip it, as I stated earlier, to something more powerful that makes me feel strong and confident. This is why I say to Do It BECAUSE You're Scared. This is an empowered statement. Again, if the result on the other side of fear is greater than you ever imagined it might be or you're proud of yourself, why are you preventing yourself from experiencing that?

I'm grateful that I woke up that day January 1, 2015, and said to myself, "I have so many fears. I am going to break through one fear a day every single day this year." And I did just that. While it might not take you a whole year of breaking through fears to change your life, it's worth it to get out there and break through maybe one or two fears a week to see what results come from it.

Will you make a commitment to yourself to intentionally break through one fear a month? It changed my life and it will change yours, too, if you're willing to allow it to do so.

Lynda Sunshine West

She ran away at 5 years old and was gone an entire week. She came home riddled with fears and became a people-pleaser. At age 51, she decided to face one fear every day for an entire year. In doing so, she gained an exorbitant amount of confidence and now uses what she learned to fulfill her mission to empower 5 million women and men to share their stories with the world to make a greater impact on the planet. Lynda Sunshine West is the Founder and CEO of Action Takers Publishing, a Speaker, 23 Time #1 International Bestselling and Award-Winning Author, Contributing Author Entrepreneur Magazine at Brainz Magazine, Executive Film Producer, and Red Carpet Interviewer.

She believes in cooperation and collaboration and loves connecting with like-minded people.

Having grown up in a volatile, physically, mentally and verbally abusive alcoholic household and marrying someone just like her dad, Lynda's voice was stifled far too long. It left her feeling suppressed, ignored, and judged, which made her shut down.

At the age of 51, she found a life coach who helped her discover that she has value and that it was time for her to share her voice and speak out loud. In doing so, she was met with praise, recognition, and acknowledgment.

Lynda Sunshine no longer sits in the back of the room, but now speaks on stages, interviews stars on the red carpet, makes tv and podcast appearances, publishes books, and creates positive and uplifting communities for her clients.

She proudly donates a percentage of her profits to Life Is Good Playmakers Project, a 501(c)(3) nonprofit.

Connect with Lynda Sunshine at

https://www.actiontakerspublishing.com/.

CHAPTER 3

Me, Myself and I

Anja Schwarz

L ooking back, it all makes sense…

"Me"

"Being alone has a power that very few people can handle." ~Steven Aitchison

---

I did not have a bad childhood; I grew up extremely protected and comparatively naïve. One repetitive issue that kept appearing in my life revolved around BEING ALONE.

Some time ago, I discovered that BEING ALONE started earlier than I remembered. It was much more subtle than what happened to Kevin in the holiday movie, "Home Alone." I was not left behind or forgotten; my life just turned out in a way that my experiences always left me feeling like an outsider.

It started when my soul entered my recent life experience. My parents were not married when my mother conceived me, and sex before marriage was a NO-NO in those days. An unborn child feels everything the mother feels, and my mother was not supposed to be pregnant; I was not supposed to be there. I was neglected and alone. However, my parents were in love and had great sex, which gifted me with a lot of love and light. Six weeks into the pregnancy, they officially walked down the aisle and could finally acknowledge my presence.

Everything went well during pregnancy until labor started. My mom was in labor for two days before getting an epidural so I could be born. My therapist later told me that this kind of labor feels like banging one's head on a closed door for a baby. The anesthesia loosened the muscles but cut the emotional bondage between my mother and me. She didn't feel me anymore, and I lost her. Birth, the most challenging experience a person must go through, was something I did by myself. This set the tone for the rest of my life.

It was only the beginning. When I was a child, every weekend my parents drove two hours to a weekend house where the whole family would gather. All the children were at least four years younger than me. Sometimes I played with the babies, but I often chose to be by myself instead. My choice. Also, as a teenager, I was not allowed to stay "home alone." I had school friends and weekend friends, but I didn't belong in either place.

What my parents chose for me were my two godmothers. One was a good friend of theirs. She somehow managed to slip out of the friendship once I was born. I have never consciously met her. The other one was my father's sister. She had marital problems and committed suicide when I was eight years old, leaving me alone without a godmother.

Originally, German, I married a Dutch guy, a merchant ship captain. He worked away from home for four months before being off duty for two months. Most of the time, I lived alone with my two children in a foreign country, where I still had to learn the language. Looking back, this was the most challenging time of my life because I felt so alone.

The more challenged I felt, the harder I worked to keep the ends together. I became a people pleaser. Logically, not without consequences. When I was thirty-seven years old, I was sure I was getting old. I had regular headaches, back pain, and allergies. When a palm reader told me this was because I was picking up energy from other people, I knew from deep inside myself that only I could do something about it. I had to take care of myself, take 'responsibility' for myself, and get out of this mess.

"Myself"

"The More You Know, The More You Realize You Don't Know." ~Aristotle

---

I learned how to strengthen my energy and boundaries with Psycho-Energetic Therapy. My development was so fast that it was hard for others to keep pace with my inner change and personal growth. Next, I discovered Applied Kinesiology, which significantly impacted my vision of the world.

My teacher, Kick, a Dutch woman, became my mentor for a short time. She was curious, enthusiastic, rebellious, and highly spiritual with a scientific background. She encouraged me to continue my research. She was as mad as a box of frogs combining spirituality and science in astonishing ways. She is still my hero, although in the meantime watching from heaven. At that time, I felt my journey started.

I was raised not believing in anything I could not touch. Now, learning about energy work, I thought I had found my kind of people. I blamed my parents for not understanding me and was relieved when I finally thought I had found the reason for constantly feeling like an outsider. After a short while, it turned out that in all the courses and workshops I took, in a crowd of weirdos, I was still an alien. My point of view was different, and others did not get me. The disappointment was huge, and I started doubting myself.

Then I thought, 'What the f...' and reconsidered. What I expressed and shared seemed so logical that I wondered why others could not see this. I kept studying various alternative healing methods. The more I studied, the more questions I had. Why would one alternative healing method work for my best friend but not me? I kept investigating, and when I found something new, I would try it on myself and work with friends and/or fans who would voluntarily serve as guinea pigs.

In the meantime, in real life, I got a divorce and changed my life completely. Everything went really well for a short time. And then I broke my foot. "Why would I break my foot?" It didn't make any sense to me. Breaking a bone means: pushing too hard, pushing yourself to a limit. I didn't realize that this was precisely what I was doing. Anyway, this was a turning point. And before it got better again, it got worse.

I became a stranger to myself. No matter how much I slept or rested, I was exhausted. My body gained weight and would not react like it used to. I felt so stuck and powerless, even with all my tools. Many times I wished that I could just go back to my former, normal self. Surprisingly, or not, that didn't happen. For six months, I worked with a personal coach. It turned out that what seemed like a big step backward was a huge step forward. I jumpstarted into the soul energy, and it felt overwhelming, exhausting, too much in every way.

"I"

"What keeps life fascinating is the constant creativity of the Soul! " ~Deepak Chopra

---

When I finally felt better and could see the invisible again, I started investigating what had hit me. It was not just one thing that happened to me. A whole lot of things came up in my investigation. At that time, I had good days and I had bad days. Generally, I felt better in the mornings and utterly exhausted in the evenings. It took me a long time to define in detail what had occurred. The only clear awareness was that I was like a sponge sucking up everybody's energy.

It was not a conscious action. Through personal development, I became more aware, sensitive, psychic, and empathetic. It didn't make me as happy as I thought it would. I kept fighting windmills. As long as I did not see anybody or do anything, it seemed okay. But being invited or going out for dinner was pure stress. "How could I protect myself? What kind of problems did others have that I needed to be aware of so I would not attract them into my energy?"

Whenever I felt devastated, I became reticent and went back to square one. I wrote down all the possibilities I knew or which came up as possibilities, inner knowledge, signs, and symbols. Then, I started to organize my ideas. I started differentiating between body, soul, mind, and spirit.

While my subtle mental and spiritual bodies seldom came up during my investigations, my physical and emotional bodies seemed to have problems all the time. I had been writing down, changing, discarding, and starting from scratch before something satisfying finally developed through what I would call 'heavenly intuition.'

I realized that every coin has two sides. Solitude encourages creativity because you are free to let your mind wander. During this time of solitude, I had the best self-talk and many AHA moments, experiencing one of the pieces of my ever-lasting puzzle falling into place.

I was excited and tried to talk to other light workers, but I could not find anyone who could understand or grasp what I was trying to say. I was alone with all this divine inspiration. I had tremendous new insights whenever I considered abandoning my self-imposed duty of finding the truth. It was my inner voice crying out: you can't stop now. Something spectacular is coming up. As a woman, it is my job to be curious. So, the self-development drug hit again. I had to go on.

"We are all in this together."

"We rise by lifting others!" ~Robert Ingersoll

During my journey, I figured many others had the same urge and issues. We all want to connect with our souls, know our purpose, and find our path. We all want to feel profoundly and make progress on our individual journeys. That is what we desire as a light worker's community. I was not alone anymore. However, I was not aware of the combined consequences. Theoretically, it was all clear, and then life came along, and issues became real.

Neither my body nor my mind could process all the intangible information I received. I remember crying in the kitchen for no reason. I was deeply saddened and didn't know why. When the kids asked me what was wrong, I had no answer. I usually pulled myself together and did what I had to do as a single mom.

30

Not all issues turned out unfavorably. I longed for a partner and met my recent husband via the internet in the next step. We both knew exactly what we didn't want anymore. We did everything we were not supposed to do according to the guidelines of good etiquette, getting to know each other. This speeded up the process enormously. We are soulmates, for sure. All my work started to bear fruit. I am not alone anymore.

Meeting a person and getting close is initially challenging for every highly sensitive, empathetic person. Feeling emotions is something we often do subconsciously. We don't acknowledge every emotion separately and don't consider that individual perceptions might differ. But when the emotion is received ten times stronger than what we are used to because we elevated our vibrational level into a developmental stage of being super aware, a normal human reaction is to fight or flight. I was in love and highly exhausted.

My feeling of empathy was magnified, too. Empathy (the ability to sense other people's emotions) was the other superpower I struggled with. It struck me when I read that our brain reacts to empathy in the same regions and in the same way it does when we experience physical pain. My brain thought I was in physical pain. A seed was planted to find a remedy.

"From woe to wow."

"Empathy is a global, contemporarily relevant misunderstanding." ~Anja Schwarz

---

From visualization and cutting cords, to carrying gemstones, I tried many things to protect myself. Everything helped, but nothing worked 100%. My power to sense other people's feelings, pains, and thoughts

31

was super intense. I was confused and had difficulty knowing what initially belonged to me and what did not.

Then I heard someone say in an interview that protection against other people's energy was unnecessary. It is part of our human experience. A great inspiration that started working in my thoughts.

I understood that our energy combines body, soul, mind, and spirit. These terms and definitions vary in different languages and topics. So, I defined the differences for clarity in my further investigation.

1. The body is inherited from our ancestors, our DNA, the physical territory where we need to move and do things.

2. The soul is forever, immortal, the emotional territory, where we need to experience and feel things.

3. The mind is our individuality, what we make of the circumstances we live in, and the mental territory where we need to understand and release.

4. The spirit keeps the body, soul, and mind together during the present lifetime and lets go when we die. It works in the spiritual territory where we can breathe and surrender.

This was the basis for an extensive system of energy root cause analysis. On body territory, no matter how old we are, there are only three to four root causes that keep initiating the same issues repeatedly in our lives. So, root cause analysis, as frequently used in science, slightly altered in its practice, is extremely effective in energy work.

There is no step-by-step manual for personal development. We don't develop linearly, but we think linearly, and that causes confusion. My personal troubles appeared to result in the transition from body to soul territory. I needed to be mindful of where and how to work with energy. The body has to become aware, and the soul needs to experience. Ignoring the slight difference might start a vicious circle. **'Been there, done that.'**

From my experience and thorough investigation of the different energetical territories, I can say that opening our soul territory involves various new tasks on a personal development journey.

Emotioning: Emotioning means experiencing emotions. Emotions can be complicated, confusing, messy, and annoying. On soul territory, this is even worse because emotions are felt much stronger. Emotional people often don't make sense and stress themselves and their social environment. Feeling emotions, checking them off, and saving them into our emotional memory, they become part of our emotional intelligence and will be recognized without irritation in future experiences. My newly discovered hobby: I am collecting emotions.

Change habits: Old-fashioned integrated habits and energy patterns don't work in the soul territory because of the higher energy frequency. For a long time, I pulled away energy from others to help them with their energy flow. I unknowingly blocked my energy flow because I was unaware I was partly working in the soul's territory, where emotioning would have been much more effective. I had to be mindful of my actions and not let myself slip into automatic pilot.

Compassion: Compassion is a great virtue. Although it might mean different things to different people, it usually includes the wish to empower the person in question by helping them. Compassion is a way of being, especially right now in this world. What we have learned from our ancestors is pity. Pity implies that the person in question is a powerless victim and deliberately kept in the victim's position. It might make your EGO feel better, but… compassion will alleviate both persons concerned. I always wanted to jump in and help, but I learned to become an observer, listener, and quiet supporter.

Self-Love and Self-Responsibility: Self-love and self-responsibility are two more essential items induced by a shift into soul territory. Self-love is the primary key to mastering the new world. It is where we come from. Can you stand in front of the mirror and say, "I love you!" Do it and feel it! Self-responsibility was more of a challenge to me. I took too much responsibility for others. I forgot about myself. Not good. The result was exhaustion until I enforced discipline and balance.

Stomach issues: Many people, me included, get stomach problems once they open up to soul energy. For three months, I could not eat meat or drink coffee. My stomach reacted so sensitively that my diet got pretty dull. I like cooking, I like good food, and I like it hot and spicy. But I had to be very careful. Without my tools, it could have turned into a disaster. I was lucky to be able to balance my stomach issues.

Conclusion: The transition between body and soul territory happens suddenly and takes a long time. I know this seems contradictory, but what I mean is that the soul territory opens up without warning. All the unknown challenges will make you want to return to your old you; at least, this was me. Going back is possible, but only in the beginning. In the end, it is not an option. Using tools and getting help to fast-forward is the way to go.

Nobody taught me how to deal with this transition into the new world. I cannot blame my parents. They didn't know. And I am pretty sure that none of my teachers knew either.

I am one of many pioneers to discover a new existence. So, I try things. I am my first guinea pig. If it works, I will look for three other people I can try to help. If that works, it goes down in my notes and ultimately will be processed and admitted to my *Fountain of Colour Empowerment* system. This system is a framework that everybody can use to see what territory they are in and how they can balance what is coming up. I still use it regularly. Mainly to help others, but sometimes I use it for myself, especially when I encounter energy vampires.

Blood is not thicker than water anymore. Family can be a burden to highly sensitive, empathetic human beings. They know you as the daughter of..., the sister from..., the cousin who... You are not recognized as an intuitive individual.

I realize that, at this moment, the world we live in is complicated for empathetic people. There is a lot of energy confusion in the transition between OLD and NEW. When I meet with my blood family, I need my clearing system, as low vibrations will drain high vibrations. I don't always need my clearing system when I am with friends. I choose my friends wisely. When more people clear their past and raise their vibration, we can look back and say: That was a developmental stage we overcame.

For a long time, I wondered why I had healing gifts, but now it all makes sense. I am paving a path for others to follow. My powers include Clairaudience, Clairvoyance, Claircognizance, Clairsentience, Clairgustance, Clairsaliene, Clairempathy, and Clairtangency. Not being able to manage them got me into trouble. In the meantime, I have become a master of my energy. If you resonate with any of the above, I am here to support you!

Anja Schwarz

Anja Schwarz is an authentic Spiritual Health Care practitioner and transformational energy seer.

She works with empaths all over the globe who are ready to take responsibility for their lives and would like to release energetic entanglements that no longer support their highest divine purpose so they can develop into the change makers so much needed in this world.

Anja brings over 20 years of experience via her transformational energy work and signature clearing system, "Empathy Empowered," for a vital and brilliant life.

Her extensive training includes, among others, Touch for Health, Kinesiology, Feng Shui, Foot Reflexology, Craniosacral Therapy, Psycho Energetical Therapy, Meridian activation, Aura reading, Reiki, Theta Healing, Akashic Record reading, Soul Realignment, Colour Balancing, and Meditation Technique.

Anja is passionate about teaching empaths DIY Spiritual Health Care at its best. Eating healthy and regular exercise is not enough in the world we live in today. Empaths, especially, need accurate tools for

Self-health-care so they don't lose their powers, lose themselves, and suffer from fatigue, overwhelm, and anxiety.

Anja was born in Hamburg, Germany, in August 1962. She has lived abroad for more than half of her life in Michigan (USA), the Netherlands, and Luxembourg. She currently lives in Spain where she enjoys life with her second husband.

She thoroughly enjoys energy work and is always curious to meet people and hear their stories. Anja is passionate about teaching people how to deal with empathy so they can use the profound knowledge they intuitively pick up about others to their own benefit.

Connect with Anja at www.fountainofcolour.com.

CHAPTER 4

Extremely Sensitive to a Strong, Powerful, Confident Woman

by Anjana Nambissan

Perhaps if you had met me a few years ago, you would have realized that this moment, this time, and this me were impossible and unimaginable. I was an incredibly sensitive person and didn't know how to process my feelings. The deepest emotional need of every human being is to love and feel loved. Growing up, I completely lost the ability to love myself. I was never good enough, so I was always self-critical. My darkest journey through major depression, anxiety, loneliness, and rejection has made me who I am today. It hasn't been an easy journey. But now, I am proud that I have learned to empower myself and become a strong and independent woman. I started to love and take care of myself, and my life became a wonderful experience. Now I'm a life coach passionate about healing and guiding others through self-love.

We are all born with this powerful mind, and sadly we were never taught how to use it to our advantage. We don't control our thoughts; we allow our thoughts to control us. We make life miserable with our thoughts. That was exactly my case until I met my life coach.

Let me tell you my life story; an inseparable mix of reality and my inner stories.

I was born into a middle-class family in India. In a patriarchal society, girls are seen as a burden and boys as a blessing. The extended family and society blamed my parents for having two daughters. I know many girls felt rejected just because they were born female. Despite everything, my parents loved me and expressed it in their way. They came from pure survival mode. I understand their perspective now, but my little self couldn't. For generations, loving children meant worrying about their future. My parents also held the same belief. They always made sure that all my material needs were met and that I got a good education, got a well-paying job, and married a nice person. My basic needs were met, so my focus was on meeting my emotional needs. My parents didn't know how to help me with my feelings, and my little creative mind kept making up stories like I'm not good enough to be loved.

Social conditioning always had a huge impact on our lives. Being a girl came with its own set of rules. Society rules our lives, and the beliefs are passed on through generations. Parents fear society. It can make or break their kid's future. There's also a heavy burden on parents. A child's good and bad behavior, successes and failures define the parent as good or bad. This doesn't change even after the child becomes an adult. It's no surprise that they acted with anger and sadness for every little mistake my sister and I made. My parents went through terrible stress and poor health because they were worried about us. One thing I really wish is to go back in time and remind them that they are wonderful and that our actions don't define them.

I'm grateful for everything I got as a child, especially when I know that girls in my parent's generation were denied even a basic education. I think the purpose of my life was to be emotionally sensitive and come out of it and show light to many.

At the age of ten, I was moved to a boarding school. It was a lovely school with excellent teachers. Participating in extracurricular activities and competitions slowly gave me confidence. Although the professors were very encouraging, I didn't make any good friends there. My fragile mind crumbled when my classmates started bullying and body-shaming me for no reason. It was difficult to comprehend, and I had no one I could rely on for support. One of the things I regret now is that I believed other people's comments and didn't realize my worth.

During that time, I became an expert at suppressing my emotions and telling myself that I was a terrible person and didn't deserve to have anything good in my life. At one point, I believed I had to compete with my sister for the love of my parents. There was constant judgment and comparison. An engineering degree put me on equal footing with my sister who studied medicine.

After graduating, I immediately started working to pay off my student loans. My past generations passed down the mindset of lack, and I believed it was not right to use my own income. Only recently did I realize that I had an unconscious pattern of sacrificing my own pleasures for the family.

Our family tradition makes us have an arranged marriage. Society and family decide what is best for us! For me, this was an opportunity to be the best daughter ever! I got married and started a new life in America with my husband.

I had this fairytale image in my head about marriage. A perfect marital life that's full of love, care, and support. My husband was a

41

very loving and caring person. But the way he showed his love didn't make me feel loved. He wasn't great at expressing or understanding emotions. I believe we should only get married when we are emotionally healthy. I entered my marriage with all the emotional scars from my childhood, and I was desperate to get my emotional needs met. Love language differences and emotional ignorance in love hurt me more and convinced me that I could expect nothing good from life.

Working as a software developer in the United States helped us financially. But the work stress took a toll on the family, which added to my mental anguish. The corporate culture was more than I could handle.

Our life went on and we were blessed with two beautiful girls. I found myself repeating the same childhood cycle with my daughters. I was stressed out from work or preoccupied with my thoughts when they needed me. I didn't know anything better. Life was getting worse day by day and I was at the point of no return. My health started to deteriorate.

It was truly a divine intervention in my life! My yoga teacher (now my dear friend) caught me when I was in an emotional breakdown and got me to talk to her life coach friend. I felt the urge to listen to her and take responsibility for my emotional health. I surrendered to God completely and started trusting the process. I learned about the creative power of our minds and how we create our inner stories. As an emotionally driven person, I had difficulty understanding the thoughts that generated my emotions. Through daily journaling and meditation, I slowly began to become aware of my thoughts. My life coach has really helped me analyze situations in my life, my feelings about them, and the thoughts behind them. I started reading a lot of self-help books and listening to audios. Louise Hay, Brahmakumaris, and VivekaVani have had a huge impact on me and helped me learn more about my mind. A daily gratitude journal was another great addition.

This also involved a lot of shadow work. I was learning about myself, finding and accepting my good and bad aspects. Every person I met had something to tell me about myself. When I disliked someone's behavior, I wrote down the traits that got me off track, and when I looked at them again, I realized it was hidden in me. I was ashamed of that side of myself and never accepted it. Life has given me the opportunity to learn about myself and accept myself. People around me held up the mirror to show me my true self. My life coach has taught me to fully love, accept and forgive myself, and live my life authentically without any masks.

While I was busy learning about my thoughts and feelings, my inner healing began. My mindset started shifting. I could see life in a new light, experience things a bit differently. Since then, I never gave up trying to improve my thinking. I started looking for patterns to learn about myself, find my unconscious patterns, and embrace my dark side.

My healing was noticeable to the people in my life. They came and talked to me with confidence about their concerns and problems. It seems that just listening to them helped them. I did not know I was giving them a safe space. That's when I felt the need to become a healer. Through my emotional suffering, life was preparing me to become the healer I was meant to be! Years of pain have led me to my life purpose! It is my passion to bring light into other people's lives and lead them to a happy life.

This realization led me to SWIHA, where I earned my life coaching certification. After opening my heart to all healing modalities, I realized that my superpower remained in life coaching. My own healing journey with a life coach proved the magical power of life coaching!

Immediately after graduating, I wanted to go out and help people, but the lack of self-confidence I had since I was a child continued to hold me back. So, I kept my job and put my certification aside. A few months later, opportunities began to emerge. A friend introduced me to Wholistic Health Alliance, a non-profit organization. At one of their events, I had the opportunity to speak about life coaching and its benefits.

It was a great start. The sessions went well and some of my old school and college friends started contacting me. They wanted the magic pill I took! I started coaching and training one of my friends every week. It seemed to help them a lot to use my own life experience to explain how our thoughts produce our emotions, which in turn become our reality. It wasn't just coaching. It was a mixture of sharing wisdom and getting them deeper into their belief systems. I was slowly discovering how to serve others.

I was still working as a software engineer and felt an emptiness while doing so. I knew I was destined to do more and make a difference in the world. In March 2022, I decided to end my corporate career and start life coaching full time. It was a huge step in my life, breaking out of my comfort zone and entering an unknown space. The last few years of my life prepared me for this courageous step.

I started working on improving my confidence and did everything possible to master my coaching skills. I attended another life coaching training course at Mindvalley/Evercoach. It was a refresher and took me to a deeper side of how to change our minds easily. This gave me a great community of coaches to share experiences and learn from each other. Each coaching conversation gave me the insight and experience I needed to evolve as a life coach.

My next step was to meet people and spread the word. My dear mentor suggested that I start by holding workshops on my favorite topics. I could feel a lot of resistance and inhibition in talking to strangers and offering workshops. But I took it as a challenge. The theme of my workshop was self-love. All my healing journeys have been about self-love. So, other than self-love, what other topic can I talk about with such confidence? Researching self-love books helped me articulate human emotional needs and ways to meet them. This led me to the next workshop on relationships and parenthood. All of this got me into the field I wanted to be, reparenting our inner child.

A common theme in both self-love and parenting workshops is core human emotional needs. Each of us needs to meet core emotional needs such as attention, acceptance, affection, and appreciation. As children, we depend on our parents and guardians for these needs. Most of us were not fortunate enough to receive it exactly as we understood it. As an adult, it becomes our responsibility to listen to our own emotional needs and meet them, and reparent our inner child to become the strong, confident, powerful person that we are meant to be.

My divine gift is to give others a safe space—a compassionate, non-judgmental space to explore their thoughts, feelings, and behavioral patterns, to embrace them wherever they are on their journey, to remind them to love and accept themselves more, to help them become more aware of their thoughts.

My family life has improved so much because of my own healing! Everything remains the same except the way I look at others. It turns out that we have an ideal image for everyone. We create pain when they don't fit this picture. We translate it into the inner stories that tell us that we are unloved and not good enough. I understood that my husband was not ignoring my feelings, but that they were unknown to him. I could see his inner child in need of my acceptance and appreciation, and I realized that we were looking for it in each other. I started giving him and my girls that safe space. The relationships and family environment blossomed! It also allowed me to forgive my parents and see their vulnerable side. As I took charge of my body and mind, my health began to improve. I now have great friendships that I cherish. I am free from my dreaded corporate career and living my dream of helping others!

I continue my inner development journey. Life gives us the opportunity to recognize our unconscious patterns and limiting beliefs. I make it my mission to accept whatever comes my way and to learn and grow from it.

When life makes you feel miserable, stop, take a deep breath, and clear your head. Please understand that it is just a thought, and you have the power to change it. Thoughts do not control us. We can control our thoughts. Deep breathing takes you away from your emotions and makes you an observer. Once you identify the thought that offended you, you have the option to think the same way or differently next time.

Transforming our lives starts with shifting our mindset! Let's heal the world one thought at a time!

Anjana Nambissan

Anjana Nambissan is a certified life coach, meditation teacher, and founder of Daffodils Bloom Life coaching. She is a wife and a mom of two beautiful girls.

She is on a mission to heal many lives through life coaching, teaching about self-love, and reparenting inner child.

She was born in a middle-class Indian family, completed her engineering degree in computer science, and had a career as a software developer for fifteen years. As a part of her healing journey, she decided to leave that career and become a life coach transforming lives.

She offers personal life coaching sessions, group coaching, and workshops on self-love, parenting, and relationships. Her workshops were presented in Non-profit organizations like Wholistic Health Alliance and Healthy Mind and Souls. She loves music, dancing, and nature.

Connect with Anjana at https://www.daffodilsbloom.com.

CHAPTER 5

Belonging

by Christiane Anna Rodriguez

"This will be our last Christmas," shouted Father through the redwood forest.

I could hear the pine needles from the freshly cut Christmas Tree hit the ground in deafening slow motion. I was twelve.

My father was gregarious, exuberant, passionate, colorful, and a poet who believed in the equal opportunity of Communism. Life was a landmine of the unknown. The Extremes. Run for cover or be ready for the latest and greatest new thing.

I am first generation of Cuban descent from a lineage of musicians, artisans, singers and actresses. My aunt, Estelita Rodriguez, made many films with actor John Wayne. My Madre, a quiet, steady force of nature and a Medicine Woman from Mexico.

Out of the gate was colorful and confusing, riddled with heated outbursts or ridiculously grand times that lasted momentarily. You learn to play dodgeball quickly or disengage, disconnect and hide.

So began the spinning out. The Beatles vibrated the airways, Dr. Martin Luther King, Jr. preached Free at Last, our President was assassinated, Vietnam lingered in the air and my spirit felt unsafe. Home felt no different.

Unwanted and unsafe became my nervous system's mantra. Music became my savior. I took my last Christmas gift and duct taped it to the front bars of my banana seat bicycle. It was a red Panasonic 8-Track player that blasted Pink Floyd's "Dark Side of the Moon" and Fleetwood Mac's "Dreams" in a constant rotation.

"Now here you go again, you say, you want your freedom" ...

It was my escape from reality and I imagined that if I rode that bike through the neighborhood enough times, I could shift the energy and bring love to the people. Maybe, just maybe, for a moment, I could dream the ultimate dream into existence. The dream of a new world where war ceased and peace prevailed. A place where the humans played nice in the sandbox and LOVE was the answer.

The day Father pronounced that we were leaving the indoctrinated religion of our family lineage and diving headfirst into a cult was met with no resistance from me. I mused, the family dynamic might change for the better. It did… for a fleeting moment.

The smoking, drinking and emotional chaos stopped for a bit. There were many new friends, traveling and gatherings that ensued. Although Mother resisted the cult initially, the social aspect took her. The cult **organization** took holidays, birthdays, celebrations, and life from us. We were told not to associate with the worldly people, which translated into "anyone outside of the society of the teachings." Adios family. All our family!

Isolation was happening under my nose, yet I was surrounded by many new people, places and things that enveloped me. Served on a silver platter and dished up steadily was manipulation, deceit, lies, control, sexual eluding and zero boundaries at the Meeting Halls. Like most things experienced in my lifetime, nothing was all bad. The **organization** had to lure us in some way. The promise of a New World where war ceased and peace prevailed probably felt good to my Father, who truly desired the best for us kids. Maybe it was the cocktail waitress at Harrah's Hotel that handed him the cult book and told him what he needed to hear at the time. Whatever it was, I was having my own experience, and for the first time I felt some sense of hope that the confusion would calm. Maybe paradise was around the corner.

The next shock to the system came when we were leaving our home in South Lake Tahoe, California, and traveling the country by van, moving on to an unknown territory. Eventually, we would find the place God wanted us to serve and settled there. That's what we had been told.

Oh' Jesus! Joseph! And Mary! Oh Wait! We are not Catholic anymore and Jesus is not God and Jehovah is the chant and we have no physical family around us and we are on a road trip to who-knows-where, going to help who-knows-who to learn about a New World order coming to town?!!!

I finished my last year of schooling in a quaint little town called York Beach, Maine. Add the shock of below freezing winters, a new home, new land to commune with and wake the senses to WHA-La New Hope. New beginnings, new friends, new people, and a new congregation.

It took a few more years before I skipped out of the cult. I was fifteen and found my own place. Freedom from chaos and confusion? It took some years to gain my equilibrium. I was out in the world filled with holidays, celebrations, drugs, alcohol and sex. Lots of sex.

There were several attempts to go back to the cult due to loneliness, isolation and mental turmoil. The teachings were embedded with my circulatory nervous system like a hot wire. It ran something like this: You are worthless, unlovable and nothing without us. You will not make it out in that world without Jehovah God, and Satan will destroy you. So began the branding, throughout the **organization.** The cult marked me as disfellowshipped and socially unfit. No one, including the family, was allowed to have any contact or association with the exiled.

Everything that I knew up to that point turned its back on me, or had it? Wasn't it me that made the choice to leave the insanity? It took years to understand that, subconsciously, I ran from the cult and the Communism mind control. Then, a few more years to unlock the cage that the men in that cult society placed me in. I held the key and didn't know it yet.

The sense of freedom was overwhelming at the beginning. My somatic body hurt as it became acclimated to silence. No longer succumbing to preachy cult messages through repeated words, songs and prayers at some meeting hall became my norm. Alone, no family or friends from the past, life was a blur for some years and clarity was being called in.

Nature became my spiritual practice. The elementals, the winged ones, the four legged, the creepy crawlers and the standing people of the birch and pine trees of the White Mountains in New England, held my heart. I reintroduced myself to the Heavens: "Hi, my name is Christiane Anna and I know you can hear me. I know there is a better way for us humans. I see it in the artistry of your creation and in my very breath. You want me, don't you?"

Nature hikes in the forest with God felt plugged in. Afterall, who else was here to speak to. There was the Big Man in the sky, Great

Spirit, Mama Gaia, Source, Universe, Divine and Holy Spirit. Included were Mary Magdalene, who I resonated with, and Mother Mary. I needed some powerhouse Divine Feminine guidance, and these were women I knew from my early Catholic years of catechism.

Some years later I produced and hosted my own local television show in New England called "Dial It In," which summed up my feelings about the higher power of love. It came down to my own sovereignty and the love that just is. The dreamy young maiden who believed George Harrison lyrics of "Give Me Love," was on spinning vinyl.

"Om My Lord

Please take hold of my hand

That I might understand you

Won't you please

Won't you?"

Through a series of heartbreaks, dis-ease, failed marriages and isolation, my attention eventually focused on self-love. This is where the juiciness of life began to flow. My first teacher showed up and this student was ripe and ready to feel deeply. Life had a synchronistic way of placing me in the middle of the river and asking me to let go and witness what wanted to be - seen. This connection was a soul contract and came in the form of bouncy, playful goofiness with big heart intelligence. This Lover showed up in a six-foot one-inch package of brilliant star gazing eyes and a smile similar to Clint Eastwood.

My deeper traumas and wounding surfaced in this intimate relationship. Love stood by my side for twenty plus years, unflinchingly.

Me, I came and went as the afraid little girl with a nomadic spirit. I ran and ran until there was no more running. He was gone. My heart stopped. We never married, not on paper, we danced with the divine existence of life, when I allowed myself to surrender and receive the joy, laughter, and passion that was present in both of us.

With death came rebirth. Douglas was dead and new life was present. I home birthed a son in the Monadnock Mountains of New Hampshire and my greatest fear of intimacy, connection, and pure innocent Love arrived in the form of a sweet soul. Heaven on Earth was here now.

Synchronistic events began to happen at rocket ship speed. Nature continued to be the wellspring from which I drew resilience and strength, and my son became my companion strapped to my back.

There was one particular day in the Fall of 2008 when I attended a small gathering at the invitation of a wise crone. She was a magical herbalist and wizard who lived in a cottage and was hosting a special guest from Teotihuacan, Mexico. He was on a spiritual vision quest from the Pyramid of the Sun.

The remembrance of this day is crystal clear at this moment. There was a calling and a hawk that traveled with me for the entirety of my drive to the intimate gathering. I was the apprentice of this wise woman of herbalism and galactic teachings, and backroads to her cottage were familiar. On that drive, I heard a distant drum beat in rhythm with my outbreath.

I was chicken skinned as I stepped out of the vehicle and the winds shifted, the leaves blew around me like a torus field. My heart and belly felt hot as I began to feel tears roll down my face. These occurrences were not rare or isolated from me with the birth of my son. However, there was a unique song of remembrance, a dance with the Divine that swept through my vessel. Where was I? My sense was another time and place, and everything stood still.

Inside, eight of us gathered as we waited silently for the Medicine Man to arrive. In this group were dear friends and companions on a path of inner discovery and alchemy and I trusted this crone who took me under her wings. We studied with the likes of Gregg Braden who bridges Science and Spirituality and the real world together, Drunvalo Melchizedek who wrote books on the Mayan Mysteries and is an esoteric researcher, Sandra Ingerman with Healing powers of the Shaman, Ram Dass, Mooji, Snatum Kaur and many more. Immersed, I loved sitting with my elder, Carolyn Kelley, and others of like mind.

When this Medicine Man from the land of my ancestors entered the room, my breath gasped and I placed my hands over my heart and cried. I don't know if the others noticed and it didn't matter. At that point of my journey, I sat with many known healers, masters, weavers, guides, mystics, philosophers across the globe and learned we are all one and on various parts of this evolutionary journey.

A message sounded from within: "Past, Present and Future here NOW!"

I told no one.

After a long day of teachings, there were offerings from the Shaman to partake in a 1:1 Healing Session as we gathered over tea. I was the only one to come forth. He spoke some English and I spoke very little Spanish. My parents' first language was Spanish and the children were taught only to speak English in the household, yet comprehend our native tongue.

I became his apprentice for the next several years and devoted myself to the teachings brought from the land of our Ancestors. He traveled to and from Mexico and from our first meeting till our last, my Remembrance of another time and place was activated. It was clear, we walked the earth as Cuandero/Cuandera Indigenous Healers.

We talked without words as our times were spent with the elementals, tending fire, calling upon the permissions & directions, tobacco Ceremony, honoring the nectar of the Cacao and the Star People, dancing with La Luna, drumming with the heartbeat of the Womb and leaving prayer bundles and song with the waters.

My healing sessions with him showed an Ancestral lineage steeped in trauma bonding, wounds, colonization and war between my Spanish and Mexican heritage. This Sacred Technology was wisdom passed down from the Scientist and Artisans of our people from the portal of the Universal Womb. I was humbled and filled with gratitude as my ancestors, known and unknown, held my heart through these teachings.

I began hosting Ceremonial Circles on the land of the Abenaki and Nipmuc peoples in the White Mountains of New Hampshire with this Curandero. 2012 and an End of a Time of the Mayan Calendar was upon us and it was apparent that the Divine Feminine energies were at a crescendo with the Patriarchal construct and our voices were rising.

My formal education in Science and Medicine was also feeling its death rattle. The Medicine Man asked me to weave my past with the present for the next seven generations. There it was! Past, Present and Future here NOW! I was to honor all aspects of myself. The humiliation, disconnect and disfellowshipping from the Cult, the Family and Communism of my younger years, and my own self depreciation were actually walking me back HOME. Each person, place, and thing played the most perfect role for me.

The Wisdom of my own Womb held a holograph of weaving from the beginning of time. I learned how to honor and hold this cauldron of truth as a scroll of key codes that could unlock the past by recognizing the present journey and clearing her path with honor for the next generation.

I learned to listen deeply to my own inner dialogue from the intuition of my gut/womb and give her a voice that could guide me and others by showing up centered, grounded, aligned and present. Trust for life became my flow, the Ancient scrolls and codes of my Womb became the Sacred Sanctuary from which I lived from.

The Womb is the generator of vitality, life force and boundless sensual and sexual power and manifestation. It births and unites the essence of our Divinity with both aspects of our inner Masculine and Feminine essence and lovingly brings us into balance with all of life.

An Evolutionary Shift in consciousness is taking place on the planet and it comes from the Ancestors of Past, into the Future, for our Present life. We are finding our center of gravity again as a spiritual nation having a human experience.

The messages are loud and crystal clear that I AM The Wisdom Keeper of my Ancestral Lineage. My death and rebirth came from within and transformed isolation, being cut-off, exiled and held outside the gates to a place of Belonging and light for a clear vision of my North Star.

The broken connections of life began to heal energetically and physically. I took my next big leap and rented space in a healing center called Living Light, LLC. The Universe had plans and after twenty plus years, I was fired from my corporate position at the Hospital Laboratory in the very month I opened my healing practice.

My fears kicked in: "How am I going to sustain my son and myself on healing sessions with no client base?" "I can't do this." "Do I really know what I'm talking about?" "Who is going to believe me?"

I was generating a great income in the corporate world, living on a forty-eight-acre horse farm, traveling and finally feeling a sense of steadiness for my son and me. Before long my one office turned into three offices and a local TV show, podcast interviews, travel, sold out Spiritual Retreats, Women's New Moon Ceremonies and circles, and working with couples regarding Sacred Sexuality, Conscious Birthing and 1:1 Healings Internationally.

I began communicating to the whole field of life and creating a resonance that vibrated out to our living oceans. The oral traditions and reverence for life deepened. I relocated to California to mend the tears in the fabric of my family's tapestry and worked with the grapevines in Carmel Valley. I taught in Big Sur and continued to gather the women and share the wisdom of my Indigenous Ancestors.

My sense of Belonging was rewiring as I brought recognition to the colonization, mass deportations, discrimination and segregation that were deeply rooted traumas passed down through the generations. The Medicine Man reminded me, "We come from the bones of our Ancestors."

We must gather our bones, sing over them and flesh out anew. The rise of the Divine Sacred Feminine is urgent, for nothing new on this planet can be birthed without women. We are the direct reflection of the Cosmic Womb at the center of the Universe and whether we have a physical womb or not, we can tap into the energy source found within.

We hold our power center to create shifts, changes, restore balance to our life, birth projects, ideas and the Future outside of us! The patriarchal construct knows our power and has burned us at the stake, raped, beheaded, exiled, cast us out with an X, dragged us through the town square and taken our children to war.

By healing our energetic womb from within, we come into alignment with all of life and awaken to the teachings of the Ancestors. Our physical temples and blood are kept sacred so we can dance with the cycles and seasons of life. The light of the Womb pulsates with love, light and flows with all of existence. This light exposes all aspects of self and asks us to look at our tapestry, witness the tears in our fabric and remember we are connected to the gateway womb portal of the whole of existence.

The Womb will ask you to die to the enormous love within and heal the past. By doing so, you become a change agent for our future generations and the present is guided by mastering your domain. There is no more seeking outside of yourself for answers or validation. Life becomes precious, sacred, honorable and asks us to create from this primordial depth of wisdom.

We are the Ancients Embodied... Past, Present and Future here now.

Christiane Anna Rodriguez

The Path of Conscious Sacred Love and Sexuality is so often unclear and unlived and few have blazed the evolutionary trail ahead of us. It takes a huge heart to walk this vision quest with a devotional spirit to the unknown.

Christiane Anna has blazed this Evolutionary trail as an Indigenous Wisdom Keeper of the Holy Grail of the Womb. She is no spiritual lightweight. She is a Humanitarian, Visionary, Artisan, Mother and Leader who brings forth the Sacred Teachings passed down through her Indigenous Ancestors. She is intensely committed to her Sacred Path of the Wombs Wisdom.

Her formal education founded her twenty plus years in Diagnostic Medicine and Science. She has produced and hosted her own local TV show, engaging the audience in Spirituality and Women's Empowerment through her Native teachings. She is the ambassador of Global Love Music, a humanitarian promotions organization that spreads the Aloha Spirit Globally. She is the Founder of Yoni Rising Healing Practice.

For the past decade Christiane Anna has been in devotion to the Sacred Technology of her Ancestors Womb Mandala Healings. She teaches workshops globally on Conscious Sacred Sexuality, Conscious Birthing, and Rites of Passage through Ritual Ceremony.

Currently, she is building a sanctuary on the Hamakua Coast of Big Island known as the Breath of God. Her signature program is called The Sacred Gateways of the New Paradigm.

Connect with Christiane Anna at Yonirising@gmail.com.

CHAPTER 6

Empathy, Nurture, Sensitivity, Protective Instinct: Are They a Gift or a Curse?

by Dina Legland

As far back as I can remember, at the fun age of five, I started kindergarten with such excitement. That summer before school started, my baby sister was born and instinctively I was compelled to take care of her. I was quite persistent in telling my mom that I was the mom, not her. At that young age, I had a deep inner feeling that my purpose here on earth is to take care of, serve, and protect others. Have you ever had that feeling when you are standing in a place and you say to yourself, "I have been here before in another life!"? That's exactly how I felt. This feeling deep down inside washed over me. Was it a sign from above, another universe or dimension in time that I felt compelled to take care of others?

When my baby sister was born, I helped feed, bath and dress her. I made sure no one got too close to her because I was the one who had to protect her. As the years went on, I found myself taking care of the kids in the neighborhood, too. For example, when they fell off their bikes or fell on the playground and skinned their knees, I was the one who cleaned their wounds and put on a BAND-AID®, making sure they got home okay to their moms and dads and explained what happened.

During my school age years and even into my teens, I always had that sense of genuinely caring for others protecting them and listening to their concerns. My friends would always look towards me for the answers to what they were worried about the most, especially if they needed to tell their parents something. At times, it made me feel like I was the adult; I am still puzzled about that one. How ironic it is that I could not tell my mom my most inner thoughts for fear of being judged and not loved.

Growing up in a family that lived close to each other (literally within a 3 block radius) who spent a lot of time together had its good and bad moments. My favorite times were spent with my grandmother and her friends. I would make sure they were okay by getting them something to drink and eat. If they dropped something, I would pick it up for them. I even held open the door when they came over for a visit. I learned many lessons because of their very interesting stories. Their life experiences spoke volumes.

When I was in my younger teenage years, especially when my Dad and I saw an ambulance, I would ask him to follow it so I could see what happened. In my head as we were chasing the lights and sirens, I would try to figure out what type of situation the person was in and how I might be able to help. I would play out the entire scene in my head as well as saying it out loud to my Dad before we arrived. He would say to me, "You need to get into the health profession. What would you want to do?"

Oftentimes, I felt like I was the one who had to do everything. I learned at a very young age to be very organized when it came to household chores. I know this may sound crazy, but it felt as if my life was meant to be this way. I felt that it was important to take care of others as well as to take care of my surroundings, the environment around me, and knowing how to do household chores was of utmost importance. I came from a family that took pride in the things we owned and cared deeply for them. What I would say is that I had a natural instinct to be able to do the house cleaning, laundry, cooking, hosting parties, and the list goes on and on.

Another gift that I feel is quite important and I wasn't always proud of for many decades is called **sensitivity**! I had an inner struggle that pulled me in many different directions with my emotions. People have made fun of me for how I could cry at a drop of hat. (What a weird phrase, "at a drop of a hat.") As a matter of fact, there were adults in my life that teased me because of it. They would say, "Let's see how fast we can get Dina to cry!" Learning how to deal with this throughout my life took many years. It tore me up inside on a daily basis. It wasn't until my 40s that I realized that this part of me was who I truly am, an empathetic, powerful woman. It didn't break me; in fact, it defined me.

I learned how to give myself the permission to show my sensitivity to others. I would cry when things were sad and cried when things were happy. Many of my patients and their families appreciated that gift within me. It made them feel like they were not alone. They had that one person who understood them during whatever situation was at hand.

After high school, I decided to go to college and become a registered nurse. After graduating college, those times of chasing ambulances led me to join the local fire department to become an EMT. I continued that gift of serving, caring, helping, and protecting others in need into my profession and volunteering in my community. As the years went on, during my 30 plus years of nursing and emergency care, I realized this gift gave me the courage to embrace marriage and motherhood by teaching both of my daughters (who are successful professionals today) how to be loving, nurturing, responsible individuals and to become who they truly want to be. I must admit, it was not easy going through the ups and downs of marriage, raising children, taking care of family members and friends, renovating a house, and having a career, along with the everyday stresses of life.

My daughters say, "Mom, why do you talk to everyone and what is it about you that all these people who are complete strangers seem to tell you every detail of their life? Do you have something written on your forehead that says tell me your life story?" My husband said just the other day to me, "You are so intune to what others need before they do."

It's funny how you can look back on your childhood and teenage years and realize that you have become what maybe you didn't want to become. It's not so bad; it's actually your TRUTH.

Taking care of others is second nature to me. It doesn't feel like a chore or nuisance. It literally feels good to help others. I never expect anything in return when I do something for someone. A lot of people say, "What's in it for me. If you gave you must receive." I don't buy that at all. I believe we should give from the heart, mind, soul, and spirit. Throughout the many relationships I've encountered, whether they were friends, co-workers, or family members, I always took them seriously. I trusted that it was a two-way street. Boy was I mistaken. I was there for others in the only way I knew, which was by just being ME. At times it felt like I swimming against the tide. I learned through some very difficult relationships that being empathetic and nurturing was hard for others to accept. The lesson I learned here was to not take it personally. People come in and out of our lives like the seasons.

Do you feel that there comes a time when these empathetic intuitive feelings to help others in need feels like a GIFT or a CURSE? There is a standing joke in my family that I have, "MIDDLE CHILD SYNDROME!" It turns out that I am the middle child and so was my Mom. I truly believe it is how I think and breathe. For many years I thought it was a curse when in reality as I've grown from a child and now as I am reaching well into my middle-aged years, I realize that this is a gift, not a curse. It's who I am truly being, who I am, who I want to continue to be. The Middle Child Syndrome are just words. We have to look deep within to see the gift that we have been granted. Mine is being a nurturing, intuitive, empathetic, and protective human being.

When I reached the beginning of my fifth decade here on this earth, I realized once again how I truly felt about my gifts. It tested my inner strength one more time, when I was diagnosed with an aggressive form of breast cancer. At that time, I was a nursing lab instructor at the college from where I graduated with my nursing degree. It's funny how things turn out. That's the day I got an unfathomable phone call that said, "You have cancer!" All I kept thinking about on the drive home from work was, "How am I going to get through this, not for me, but for my husband, my children, my family, my friends, even my students and co-workers. That instinctive intuitive empathetic part of me that didn't want to nurture myself felt strongly about wanting to nurture those around me. You may be asking yourself, "How could she feel that way when she was faced with a life-threatening disease? She seems to be more worried about taking care of others than herself." The reason this is true is because that was my biggest FEAR. I was truly afraid of not being loved and being judged by others because I had to take care of myself first. That fear paralyzed me in a way that is not understood by many people. It truly goes back to the beginning when I was five years old. Those moments of being teased, the feeling of not being loved, being that sensitive person who only wanted to care for and protect others over myself came full circle on how I felt at that moment in a time where my life was being turned upside down. Today I am in remission and that journey through breast cancer is what I would say is the cherry on top of the sundae. You may say, "What the hell is she talking about? How can a diagnosis like cancer be good and enjoyable like a sundae?" It provided me with the ability to look at life through a different lens. Learning the appropriate tools that worked allowed me to see what I needed in order to look back at life's trials and tribulations from childhood to present day. I've come to learn and realize that these gifts of empathy, compassion, nurturing, protecting and even sensitivity were given to me from a higher power. It's my purpose here on earth to empower, support, educates, inspire others to find their gifts within themselves.

Today as a registered nurse, certified transformational health and life coach, I have taken my gifts and turned them into what I call life-saving strategies. I am the founder of Wellness Warriors for Life, LLC and I am known by my clients as, "The Inner Warrior Coach!"

Our fears can impact how we make decisions and be incapacitating both physically and emotionally. Living consistently with our fears can feel like it's "sucking the life out of us," removing the joy from our daily existence, causing physical symptoms we aren't noticing, and making us more vulnerable to disease. Identifying the toxicity of our fear at its source is the vital step to overcome what we dread most. When we discover the tools to conquer that fear, we redesign what that looks like, ultimately unleashing our inner warriors!

Dina Legland

Dina Legland is a Certified Life and Wellness Coach who uses her personal and professional experience to help clients conquer their fears to achieve a lifestyle filled with joy, freedom, and inner peace. As the founder of Wellness Warriors for Life, LLC Dina is a Wellness Warrior, Registered Nurse and EMT for over 30 years.

Dina spent her professional life taking care of others by treating home care patients as a field nurse, children as a public-school nurse and as a home care agency director. She exemplifies what it means to be a strong, courageous leader in the community. Helping others is simply a part of who she is.

As the Inner Warrior Coach, she educates people to face their greatest fears, transforming them into being empowered and confident. Dina is uniquely qualified to support others to release their fears given her own personal struggles with debilitating fears and how she overcame and mastered it. As a cancer survivor and thrivor, Dina always says, *"Cancer Saved My Life, and My Fears Almost Killed Me!"* Her journey and experience of battling and being victorious has contributed to her passion and purpose. Her mission is to share her experiences, wisdom, tools, strategies, and humor to conquer uncontrollable fears, and to seek inner wellness with freedom guilt free.

When not working with clients, you can find Dina on podcasts and speaking to organizations around the world. She loves exploring nature trails, dancing to live music, walking on the beach, and tasting wine at vineyards with her husband of 34+ years and two daughters.

Connect with Dina at www.wellnesswarriorsforlife.com.

CHAPTER 7

-------◦◦◦◦◦-------

Everyone Is a Healer

by Dina Sabnani

Though this book is about women with healing gifts, everyone is a healer and can cultivate the skills necessary to truly change their reality. Growing up in a spiritually open household, I didn't realize for a long while that others weren't aware of some of the truths I was exposed to. Though born into a Hindu household, my parents weren't the religious sorts, and my father was the head of a spiritual congregation that was very forward thinking in its approach to life and living. I grew up learning that race, religion, caste, creed, and color didn't matter, that one shouldn't judge another on their way of dress, hair, food, etc. and that at the end of the day we all belonged to a Creator of All That Is, a formless God. As a Nirankari (one who believed in a formless God), when we met others, we literally bowed to the divine within by touching their feet regardless of age, gender, social status in a way that supported the belief we are all divine.

Home for me was Hong Kong. I was educated in the British education system and had a variety of friends from all different backgrounds. I was always the 'happy chick' at school, not one of the 'cool kids' and not a nerd either, but I got along with most everyone. My parents didn't place a lot of restrictions on me, that perhaps my cousins had being 'good Indian children' but allowed me to be my own person without the conservative ideologies that come with the culture. In my teen years, they had a semi-precious crystal business and would travel to Tucson for the annual gem show, hanging out with the hippies, crystal healers, and other 'new-agey' type folk. At the young age of fifteen, my mom encouraged me to do my first healing course over a three-day weekend called Mahikari. There I learned to channel energy through my hands, recite a Japanese prayer, and send that energy to a receiver's third eye area.

I was considered a black sheep in the rest of my rather large family. My mother is one of twelve children and I have twenty-seven first cousins on that side and my father's side is much smaller with only six other cousins. It was always an interesting dynamic with my relatives because I didn't fit into their box and created a lot of cognitive dissonance. Even the way my dad 'allowed' my mom to be herself caused a lot of tension in our circles because, culturally, women were supposed to be subservient to their men, dress modestly, not work, etc. and my mother was nothing of the sort! She was a firecracker that to me seemed so completely opposite of my much calmer, serene, spiritual dad.

Needless to say, in hindsight, growing up was rather interesting!

I was daddy's girl, his sunshine and best friend. He was my mentor, guide, and biggest fan. He allowed me to be me. He would always tell me to 'never lose my bubbles' and he'd get told off for spoiling me with so much affection. He passed away when I was only twenty-seven, but I carry his wisdom with me to this day. When I was very young, I would see him counsel others in our community. If someone was sick, he'd ask for a glass of water and pray over it and ask them to drink it. Only much later did we learn about how water can be charged with words, prayers, etc. He would read people's horoscopes and palms and even match horoscopes for families that would come to him to see if potential partners for their children were good astrological matches. He had a penchant for learning about different religions, philosophy, and he made spirituality very practical for everyday use.

During a lunch date with my father when I was younger, he imparted something to me that still resonates today. He said the world was created for me, a sentiment echoed in modern day books on self-improvement, manifestation, and healing, that I was the writer, producer, cinematographer and star of the movie of my life, and I got to choose what I wanted to experience. He also said that I should always do what makes me happy and joyful. It didn't matter what anyone else thought because someone would always have their perspective/story on things, but that as long as I wasn't doing anything that was done with the intention to cause harm to another, to follow my joy. This is how I chose to live my life in the decades that followed.

Having been exposed to so many spiritual concepts so early on in life, nothing seemed weird or woo-woo to me. I understood that we were the creators of our own reality, that we all had the power to heal, that life was an experience we as spiritual beings were having, and that a belief in something greater than ourselves were the keys to life. My religion was love and being a good human being. These concepts helped me go through some truly painful times, from health issues, to losing my dad, to a disconnected relationship with my mom, to relationship failures.

Along the way, I had opportunities to take so many different and diverse healing modalities. To be honest, it was something that I naturally gravitated towards. I was always the person folks would come to for advice. I had friends calling me up to send them 'good vibes' for job interviews and was known for my positive outlook and optimism. From Japanese healing arts to Indian teachings of chakras, past lives and mantras to oracle readings, shamanic practices to Reiki and weekend workshops in between, to becoming a certified ThetaHealer™. Over a decade ago, I dug deeper into my ability to embrace new concepts and healing modalities.

During my on-again, off-again five-year relationship, I experienced ThetaHealing™ sessions and even had my ex do one to see if it helped us. This is what finally helped me identify my limiting beliefs which caused drama in my then relationship. I took ownership, cleared the issue, and assumed responsibility for my actions. After numerous attempts to make the long-distance relationship work, I finally reached a point where I could acknowledge that it wasn't serving either of us. It was then that I made the decision to walk away. I didn't realize how much I had changed until his sisters pointed out how energetically different I was.

I flew back home to Hong Kong with my tail between my legs, nursing my broken heart. I had no idea what to do next with my life and a friend of mine told me she was about to teach a beginner's ThetaHealing™ class in Dubai and to come join her. I previously lived in Dubai, but it was a bit too far, although it got me thinking. I soon found a class that was happening the next month in Thailand. Divine synchronicity. My mother surprised me and told me to go ahead and do it and that she'd pay for it.

This is how my journey into this modality began.

During the classes, I found myself thinking "How is this even possible?" "I don't know how to heal people or scan them." I remember being asked to 'see' someone's angels and I was like "Yeah, ok, sure,"

74

but I allowed myself to get into a theta state and simply tune in and I received a name and saw an image. David was a blonde haired, blue eyed male presence and I heard Mother Mary. When I shared this with my healing partner, she burst into tears and told me how she wanted to name her child David, how that name has always been so dear to her, and that Mother Mary was someone who brought her a lot of comfort in trying times. I was quite stunned as I felt I was making it up, but there were so many more moments of incredible occurrences while learning how to truly connect and become a channel for the energy.

After completing the basic, advanced, and manifesting course over a week's time and being in awe of what I had experienced in my own healing and helping others heal, I stayed back to do a fifteen-day Intuitive Anatomy course and continued to be blown away by what I was able to see, sense, feel and heal! I continued this journey by taking more courses in this modality. I flew to Idaho Falls to learn from the founder herself and dig deeper into my own healing while connecting with like-minded souls who were also drawn to learn how to become healers.

A decade plus later and I am still using these skills. Every time I work with a client, I am grateful to have learned healing techniques that allow me to truly tap into their subconscious minds and help them identify the beliefs that no longer serve them through permission based energy and belief work. I have been able to see clients from all over the world and have helped folks experience their own transformations by helping them uncover these limiting beliefs and changing them.

Funny thing though, healing never became the career I was expecting and it hasn't been a straight path for me and my journey till now. I literally could write an entire book on the adventures I have had in 'being' me! Having been born in the Philippines, raised in Hong Kong, and living/working in California, New York, and Dubai while working in a variety of jobs from retail to recruitment to client services and even heading up the marketing department for a leading fashion retailer with a million-dollar budget to stints in network marketing. I even ran two Happiness Clubs: One was in Dubai (which garnered me newspaper and magazine articles as well as TV and radio interviews) and another one in Hong Kong.

In 2015, I had the blessing to travel with my Guru to Australia and New Zealand for an incredibly blissful trip. After that, I went back to Dubai for one of my best friend's wedding and post that I decided to take a trip back to the U.S. I hadn't been back for over two and a half years. What was supposed to be a summer vacation for a couple of months turned into traveling across the U.S. and Canada for almost a year and a half. During that time, I was invited to South Texas to be a speaker for my aunt's Infinite Love healing center. I spoke to groups, led a guided visualization, and proceeded to see fifteen or so people for healing sessions on my first visit. I came back a couple of times and saw perhaps another twenty plus people as I continued my travels. Little did I know that I would end up making the Rio Grande Valley my home a year later and I have been here since October 2016.

When I officially moved here, I assumed I would have a thriving healing business and finally be living my purpose. But that wasn't the case. For whatever reason, I would see clients every now and then and had to take up a job as a server in a locally-owned dining establishment. I made some friends and life was simple. Deep inside I knew this wasn't quite it and that the Universe had other plans for me.

And it sure did.

Fast-forward to post-pandemic, after investing in my own healer/coach to really help me overcome imposter syndrome and the funk I was in, I was able to claim my purpose as being a '*lighthouse of joy*' and

76

understanding that my presence had the ability to shift other people's energy. I doubled-down on my gifts, stepped into who I knew I was, and started attracting clients for 'soul-sessions' to help them reclaim their own joy. I also created a signature workshop called the Happy Hour, which incorporates laughter therapy, mindset work, and guided visualizations and have been hired by municipalities, organizations, and businesses to speak and lead workshops as *The Joy Activator*.

I continue to attract clients who are READY for what I like to call a universal kick in the booty. They know they are meant for more, but realize they have stuff that isn't allowing them to truly become the best versions of themselves. They are willing to take self-responsibility for their lives and are willing to do the healing work required. My clients usually have gone to therapy/counseling but haven't had breakthroughs.

As a personal development junkie, I continue to develop my leadership, speaking and healing skills by taking workshops and courses that I gravitate towards. Health and wellness have become super important to me, and I continue my education in the field of human optimization and bio-hacking, understanding that it HAS to be a body, mind and spirit approach to healing and well-being. To me, it's about practical spirituality and making it easy to understand for the everyday person.

I realized that although there may be folks that are naturally highly gifted with psychic abilities, healing powers, and divination skills, anyone can learn to tap into their own innate gifts by a) believing that it is possible and b) practicing. This is where tapping into your own resonance of what feels true to you comes in and really questioning your beliefs, especially religious ones, that you were raised with in order to give yourself permission to expand your awareness of what is truly possible.

Since this book is in your hands, you obviously have an interest in developing these gifts for yourself or at least a healthy curiosity, which is what you need to in order to begin your own journey of tapping into your own innate powers. How do you begin? I recommend looking in your area for workshops, courses and/or seminars on different healing modalities. If you live in a town that is not too plugged in, get online. There are literally hundreds of thousands of resources online for you to start your own journey.

It's about trying different modalities and seeing what feels right, what resonates in your beingness. The best way of really doing this is by doing a session yourself and seeing how you feel after and the clarity you gained about your own situations. Each practitioner is going to have a different energy. Some you will be attracted to and others will turn you off. This is step one in becoming more in-tune with your own instincts.

Here are some tips to deepen your ability to clear your channels and become more open to your own energy, instincts, and healing abilities.

- **Connection** - Have a connection to something greater than you. Be it God, Universe, Source, or the Creator, the terminology doesn't matter. It is the ability to trust and have a faith in a power that is greater than simply human energy. Connect with nature. Nature has a powerful healing energy that can help to balance and revitalize our bodies and minds. Take a walk in the park, spend time in the forest, or simply sit outside and enjoy the beauty of the natural world. As you connect with nature, you'll start to feel more grounded and at peace.

- **Belief** - Believe in yourself and in the concept of healing, miracles, and magic. Believe that anything is possible and that everyone has the ability to tap into their own gifts. Without self-belief and a desire to learn and expand your own abilities, you won't get very far in this journey!

- **Mindfulness** - Cultivate your innate healing powers to become more mindful of your body and your thoughts. Take a moment each day to sit quietly and focus on your breath. Pay attention to the sensations in your body and notice any areas of tension or discomfort. As you become more aware of your body and your thoughts, you'll start to notice patterns that may be contributing to any health issues you may be experiencing.

- **Meditation** - By spending time learning how to meditate, tuning out the external *noise* and tuning into yourself, you can begin to *listen* to the internal awareness that we all possess. This takes practice, but once you begin, it gets easier and you get better at it! There are so many ways to meditate. Explore a variety of them and see what works best for you.

- **Self-care** - Self-care is essential for healing. It's important to take care of your physical and emotional well-being by eating well, getting enough rest, and practicing stress-reducing activities like yoga or meditation.

- **Attitude** -Having a positive attitude is essential for healing. Believe in your ability to heal and surround yourself with positive people, thoughts, and energy. Energy is LIFE. It's also important to release any negative thoughts or feelings that may be holding you back.

- **Intuition** - Your intuition is your inner guide, and it is always trying to communicate with you. Listen to your intuition when making decisions about your health, and trust that it will lead you in the right direction. The more you trust it and tap into it, the stronger it gets. Like anything else, it takes practice and trust.

- **Gratitude** - Be grateful always. Gratitude is a powerful healing tool. Take time each day to reflect on the things in your life that you are grateful for, and you'll start to notice a shift in your attitude and energy.

- **Experience** - There are many different healing therapies available, and it's important to find the one that works best for you. Some popular options include massage therapy, acupuncture, and energy healing. These therapies can help to release blocked energy and promote healing in the body.

- **Learn** - Once you have found what YOU resonate with in terms of healing modalities, take a deep dive into it by taking courses to learn how to practice that art. It could just be for your own healing or you could then decide to become a practitioner and make it a career.

My intention by you reading this chapter is that you realize there is no such thing as coincidence. You needed to read this and tap into your own healing gifts because your light is needed in this world. The more people who heal themselves and become clearer channels to help others, the more we GET to raise the vibration of this beautiful planet we call home. As The Joy Activator, I have learned that by doing the work to heal ourselves, we can LEARN to set our default to JOY and begin to co-create a life that is beyond what we ever dreamed of.

Don't ask yourself what the world needs; ask yourself what makes you come alive, then go do that. Because what the world needs is people who have come alive! ~Howard Thurman

---

Dina Sabnani

Dina Sabnani - The Joy Activator, is a soul coach, writer, transformational speaker, and human connector. A citizen of the world, Dina's primary purpose in life is to make the world a better place by allowing people to be authentic and providing them with the skills to live a joyful life.

In 2012, Dina became a Certified ThetaHealer, where she has worked with clients on limiting subconscious beliefs and enabling them to see their greatness.

Over the past decade, Dina has conducted healing and meditation sessions that have helped hundreds of people with their emotional, physical, and spiritual issues. Dina is currently a keynote speaker and workshop facilitator who provides strategic happiness workshops for staff and leaders in the small business, non-profit, education and municipality sectors.

Dina is a reputable happiness thought leader and public speaker who has led emotional wellness workshops, and conducted presentations in over ten countries on topics including spirituality, self-love, and gratitude around the world, helping people improve their emotional

81

intelligence and reclaim their joy. She has been a UAE Ambassador for International Happiness Day and founded Dubai's first Happiness Club which garnered her media publicity.

Dina's commitment to her community has catapulted her to many leadership roles with local organizations in the Rio Grande Valley. As a self-proclaimed personal-development junkie, she continues to expand her healing and speaking skills, especially in the areas of well-being.

In her spare time, Dina is a travel enthusiast and likes to explore different cultures and food. She also enjoys making new friends through the many local events she attends. She enjoys living in South Texas with her partner and has immersed herself in the local culture with a newfound love for country music and tacos.

Connect with Dina at www.dinasabnani.com.

CHAPTER 8

Left Behind, Again and Again

by Gail Kraft

Trauma digs deeply into your heart, your soul, your body, and your mind. It can have its roots in ancestral rituals, societal norms, or events that drastically impact your life.

And then this trauma affects your choices and how your life unfolds.

Not feeling wanted, abandoned, and isolated due to feeling disconnected resulted in me putting up defenses, growing angry, and feeling worthless.

I was alone in this world.

"Even in the context of suffering – poverty, violence, human rights violations – not belonging in our families is still one of the most dangerous of hurt."
~Brené Brown, *Braving the Wilderness*

For me, these are the wounds that cut deeply as a child and went unacknowledged and buried for most of my adult life. I longed to fill this hole I didn't understand, begged to belong someplace, and was desperate to feel nurtured and cared for.

I was that person who buried this pain so deeply that it took years to even know it existed before it could heal. Recognizing that my choices were skewed due to longing to belong did not happen until I became a healer myself. As an empowerment master, I worked with clients on releasing their trauma and healing their wounds so they could move forward in their lives. I practice what I preach and so the layers of defense and anger and frustration began to slip away.

And then it came up!

It was while I was in the process of healing others with abandonment, low self-esteem, and feeling lost in their lives that I uncovered my own complex story and my own long-awaited healing.

I began my journey into personal development at the age of 21. It started with meditation and psychic training. In this process, I focused on helping others find balance, heal physical and emotional wounds, and resolve their issues, while working on my most obvious blocks.

It was at this time I was first confronted with harboring abandonment. I was pretty self-confident (I thought) and a powerful person. I went after what I wanted, and no one got in my way. Obviously, there was no abandonment here.

I had forgotten about being confronted with this observation and years later I stepped into the world of consulting as a process and project manager contractor. I became certified as a business coach and realized that there was a gap in my training.

Without people on board first, no matter how great the system or process was, it would fail. So, I decided to get this thing called a "life coach" certification.

BAM!

Holy cow, this was my calling. I was so drawn to the processes for healing and guiding that I dropped everything and went full in. I grew my practice and expanded my training for years with T. Harv Eker Money Mindset training, Neuro-Linguistic Master training, Elite Life Coach Training, Train the Trainer, Soul Realignment, and so on. I dug deeper, learned and practiced more profoundly the trade of emotional healing, and I used these tools on myself. I knew that I needed to leave my wounds behind when I worked with clients and show up for them, so I was relentless on my quest to understand my own pain and heal.

One tool I use is a process to work with your subconscious mind. By this point, I had taken down most of the defensive walls I had built throughout my life, but there was something still there. I wanted to understand what had happened to me so that I could heal it, forgive it, and move past it.

Little did I realize that a chain of events would open up that I had totally blocked from my conscious mind.

My abandonment issues began at conception and repeated over and over again in my life, deeply anchoring in the pain and loss.

And so, the process of peeking into the shadow of abandonment began.

Before going to bed, I gave my subconscious mind a job to do while I slept. I told myself that I was not going off into a free-for-all dreamland but wanted to gather the information I needed to bring down the wall in my way and heal the undefined loss I was feeling my entire life. By this time, I had become pretty powerful in directing my mind and listening to what my body was telling me.

When I awoke the next morning, I sat up with a flash.

This began at conception! Not only was I not wanted then, but this also continued with a repeating pattern throughout my childhood.

At Conception

The flash that woke me up indicated that at conception my mother tried to abort me. I'm here, so you know she failed. In order to validate this information, I met with one of my older sisters.

Over coffee I asked, "So, mom tried to abort me?" Her response?

"How did you know that? You're some kind of witch!"

I laughed. No, you see, trauma stays in your body and I asked about what was going on with why I was angry, didn't trust, and felt a loss in the pit of my stomach. I got the answer.

So I began to get curious about what else happened that I was not facing and that has anchored deeply this feeling of loss.

Death and the Nightmares

I was the last of 9 births. I had three sisters who were married and nephews older than me when I was born. The siblings at home were teens and by the time I was three, they were all working or also out of the house.

Mom worked downtown Boston and left for work one day. She never did return as this is where she died from heart failure. I remember going to the grave and I remember the pain and sadness of the family, but I did not yet understand that mom was never coming home.

What did I do wrong?

How can I fix this?

Where do I fit in now?

What is happening to me?

That's when the nightmares began…

Mom and I are at the Roxbury Crossing train station in Boston heading into town. The train comes, I get on and turn to see mom still on the platform as the doors close. At this age, I only know how to go to Downtown Crossing and turn around to get back.

I remain on the train feeling more and more anxious as I impatiently wait for the train.

Finally! I get off the train and head back. Each click of the train wheels, each station door opening, each flash of lights from the tunnel passing remind me that it is taking too long.

I get to the station, and no one is there. I am alone.

Abandonment issues? Who, me?

This nightmare continued until I was 13 when I purposefully shut this down.

Dating Patterns of a Widowed Dad

Father issues, well that is another chapter, but he plays a huge roll in anchoring in my feeling of not belonging here. He was now a single man who worked nights, leaving me alone after school to fend for myself. He was a man looking for a mate.

I would hear him talking with his latest girlfriend and express how horrible his life was. Here he stood, having to play both father and mother to this young girl, and he was saddled with having to care for someone after his other children had grown and moved out.

Saddled with this child.

This is when I became friends with shame for being responsible for the death of my mother and being responsible for the position that put my father in.

I was ashamed of the fact that I was a burden, that I was responsible for my mother's death and a burden on my father.

I would dial random numbers on our phone until a woman would answer. I would ask her if she had a spare mother so I could make our family whole again.

No one had one to spare.

Abandonment issues? Who, me?

By the time I was 13, I was a gang kid, finding family wherever I could.

The Final Stab

The summer I turned 13, I had one sister still around who would, from time to time, take me under her wing. She got married and had a baby. That summer, I moved in with her and her family, baby-sat for a neighbor, and lived a pretty peaceful life for the first time ever.

And then, the end of summer came, and I watched in shock as the movers came and took this family away. I was 13 and did not speak to or see this sister again until I was 36. She had simply disappeared from my life.

I was so heart-broken that I couldn't even speak. What did I do wrong, again? How could this be happening? What was I to do next?

And then I arrived back home. There, my father stood across from me, almost toe to toe, and said, "Well, now what are you going to do? You're all alone now."

And that is when the nightmares stopped.

And that is when the walls were cemented.

And that is when the decision to rely on no one ever again took root.

I SHUT DOWN!

What I didn't realize is that this is when I began looking for family, looking for belonging, looking for validation that I matter.

Choices of the Wounded Child

I began hanging with the local gang the following summer and came home just before my father returned from work at midnight. I was on my own. I relied on friends and the "gang" for information and validation. I was tough as nails and took no nonsense from anyone.

This, finally, was family. We watched out for each other and made sure we were safe. We also were tied to this group. No dating outside the gang, and no hanging elsewhere. This was where you belonged, period.

Then at 16, a series of events pushed me out of my father's house. I was to choose which sibling I was to live with, even though most of them I had seen only once in my life. I chose to move in with my brother and his growing family in the suburbs.

The good news was that this got me out of gang life. It was confusing for a while, but I got a job and began planning my release. I wanted to know what living on my own was all about and make my own choices. I moved out on my own at 19, supported myself, and began to learn what life was all about.

I'll touch slightly on the choices I made that were based on the feeling of abandonment as there are so many and all so interesting.

Two marriages and both rooting in falling in love with the family.

The first was with my boyfriend from the age of 14 and was very short-lived. I adored his older brother and was mesmerized by his matriarchal mother. However, both he and I were too young and too naïve to understand what working on a relationship was all about. I hung on for a while because I did not want to lose family, but when my daughter was 1 1/2 years old, I moved out on my own once again.

The second relationship lasted 23 years and I never fit in with the family. I tried to insert myself into the hierarchy of six other girls, but found myself left out and pushed out. I tried to make my own rooted family, really working at it, really pushing to make this one successful. What did I know about the family unit, healthy boundaries, and when behavior is not cool?

Many tears and many years later we split, my daughter was married, and my son enrolled in graduate school. I decided to move across country to San Diego. I had family there, so maybe this was where I belonged.

Here is where we get into work and how my career had been driven by the need to be validated and recognized for making things right. I was determined to prove myself worthy, be the best at what I did, and sought validation along the way.

When I lived on the East Coast, I pushed really hard at work to make change, meet objectives, and achieve things no one else was able to do. I was very successful in my career, easily moving to top management positions. You see, being abandoned myself, I was super vigilant about being sure my teams felt safe and had what they needed to succeed. They succeeded so I succeeded and got the recognition I thought I needed. It was a safe haven and a sure win.

I moved from job to job still seeking love and belonging and although I achieved my goals, received bonuses and promotions, and got the recognition I was looking for, I still needed to go home and face me. Then I moved from the East Coast to the West Coast.

Although by now I was meditating and doing some form of personal development, I found myself in a company that did not match my values and was totally wrong for me. I knew this day one, and yet chose to stay. I was strong. I was smart. In the past, I had turned failures into successes. I was responsible to make things right, so I needed to make this work.

The short story is, I got fired. I knew it was coming and also understood the politics behind why. However, termination and abandonment go hand in hand. I was being triggered all over the place and was totally out of control. Crying, migraines, nausea, you name it.

And then the hammer dropped, and I spiraled into anger, hurt, revenge, blame, and one friend said I was totally in PTSD mode. Like all chaos, this was one of the many wakeup calls I have had in my life and I am so grateful for this.

I became so angry that I found a lawyer and was pursuing legal action. It was during this process that I got up one morning, looked in the mirror, and thought, "I don't like who you are, and I am surprised you have any friends."

I chose to go for a settlement and stop the suit against this company, became a contractor for process improvement, and got certified as a business process improvement coach. After that training, I realized the people skill portion was really lacking. After what I had gone through, I believed I needed to enhance my communication skills, so I decided to get this thing called a "life coach" certification to fill that gap.

Holy cow! This is why I am on this earth! The philosophy of life coaching is the same that I used as a manager of successful teams: listen and show up with what they need.

As I learned more and more about the human mind, the conscious, subconscious, and the superconscious, the trauma responses and body connection, ancestral trauma, and so on, the more I learned about myself, the greater value I brought to my clients.

As I learned, I healed, and as I healed, I connected with more and more people looking to connect with and heal that "inner child's" pain.

And my walls came tumbling down. I began to understand who I am and why I am here. I started to find and then speak my truth while helping others do the same. I was becoming whole again.

And then that night came when I asked, what is this last block of the wall I have been taking down? Why won't it move? How can I better understand the love that is within and allow myself to heal? This is a stubborn one.

You hear so often talk about the inner child and that phrase can seem so elusive. That part of you never leaves and it is that part that is looking to heal and looking to be loved and validated.

Looking for acceptance, support, nurturing, and love.

The child-self remains alive, and we each own the responsibility to care for and heal that pain. S/he is looking to you for help.

I know I was nervous about facing this demon at first and if I had not already been a coach I probably would have been very nervous about facing the stories I had hidden away, locked in my psyche, and housed in my body. But the closer I got to understanding the circumstances and closer I got to resolving the trauma and healing the wounds I had carried for so long, the easier it got.

After uncovering the many examples of feeling abandoned as I grew up, I intentionally began the healing process. I sought help with an Indian medicine man and, while in a sweat lodge, I thought about my mother, her circumstances, her available choices, and what was and was not within her control. I told her I would probably have made the same choices given her circumstances, and truly forgave her and forgave myself for holding on to anger.

I met with a coach and worked on understanding my father, his limited understanding of consequences, and doing the best you can with the tools you have. I actually felt empathy and forgave him for he did not know what the impact of his actions would be.

I now lean in when something comes up, curious about the root of what I am feeling, and determined to understand and release the pain, walking away with the lesson and the gift. I get in touch with my very core, embrace my personal truth, and live in alignment with what feels right.

The inner child holds on to the pain but also holds *innocence, play, wonder, curiosity, creativity, honesty, imagination, and laughter.*

Using a gentle approach to uncovering my wounds, meditating, mindful living, conscious choices, integrity, and accountability, I am able to easily release new traumas that show up and lovingly care and nurture that inner child. I do this for me but, more importantly, I do this for healing those I work with and those I love. It is an empowering process.

Gail Kraft

Gail Kraft, Motivational speaker, podcaster, radio broadcaster, author of *The Empowering Process*, and empowerment master comes from an inner-city background and a history in corporate where she helped businesses achieve their goals with clarity of vision using her street-smart grit.

She entered into her own coaching business in 2012, creating a model for success for leadership and individuals ready to find purpose. Her approach is to guide you into gaining higher self-awareness, creating smarter goals, and lowering stress by making conscious choices while taking control of your life today. Clients that partner with Gail shift from feeling unfulfilled into living purposefully, move from uncertainty to clarity, and change perspective from living lost to living life fully.

Connect with Gail at http://gailkraft.com.

CHAPTER 9

Being a Caregiver

by Janet Ward

As I continue this journey called life, I look back on all the trials my friends and family have been through and I ponder how I always find myself as the caregiver.

I have learned many ways to be a caregiver and still be happy within myself, to love myself first, to be there for the ones I love, to take care of their needs and still take care of me.

I married at a very young age and had three children close together. It didn't take long for me to realize how poorly equipped I was to be a mother, to be all that they needed emotionally, and give them the nurturing they needed.

Fortunately, they did flourish in spite of my inadequacies, excelled in school, and became loving and caring adults. They all became registered nurses as well as wonderful caregivers and parents.

My first experience as a caregiver outside my home was of my dad as he struggled through his last years with Parkinson's disease. Parkinson's affects the synapses in the brain and creates gaps that interrupt the transmission of the appropriate receptors in the brain. As his disease progressed, him not knowing who I was or anyone else made it very hard for him as well as for my mother who was already in her advanced years. My dad was a hard-working farmer who became an invalid. He spent many nights and days tormented by the fact that he would never get any better. At that time, I stepped in and spent as much time with them as possible, taking care of my dad's needs and helping my mother. After about three years of Parkinson's, he would sit and cry. He wasn't able to accept all that was happening to him. These were very hard years for my family and I in our attempts to help him through these tough times. The denial, the depression, the hopelessness was almost unbearable. My mother's struggles became harder, trying to help him get up and down, change his clothes, and cook for him. Therefore, my time with them kept increasing. I spent a lot of my time taking care of his emotional needs and reassuring him, trying to keep hope alive.

By the fifth year, he was basically bedridden and our family and my mother had to make the hard decision to put him in a nursing home so he could get twenty-four-hour care. And, my mother needed care and comfort also, reassurance that we had made the right decision. Out of love and determination, I did it. My parents were married for sixty-seven years. His death devastated her, disabling her ability to function for a while. His death was also very hard for me. My dad was my hero, my idol, the one I always turned to for advice and protection.

When my children were teenagers, I remarried to a wonderful man and that took a lot of pressure off of me and my children. I was able to stop working seven days a week, freeing up more time with them.

After two years of marriage, I fell into the caregiver role again. My husband had several failed back surgeries and with the debilitating pain he was forced to retire. He was a strong, healthy man with a great career and it was very hard for him to sit at home in pain. He developed diabetes and, after several years of noncompliance, it damaged his heart. That eventually led to a heart attack and heart failure. He had bouts of deep depression and felt like a burden, a failure, and inadequate as a man to take care of his family. How could I possibly reassure him? It was a struggle to find little ways to help him get through each day. What could I do to prevent him from getting into an even deeper depression? I would get him interested in small outings, entertained close friends, taking him to visit with his family that he dearly loved, and talking him into staying with his parents for short periods of time. I bought a motorhome to travel with him after he couldn't fly anymore because of his heart failure. As a caregiver, we must be creative and think about their needs and what will make them happy.

After thirty-two years, he got into some irreversible health situations that couldn't get any better and he passed away. It was devastating and it took me a long time to accept that he was gone forever.

Even before my husband passed away, one of my brothers developed Parkinson's disease. Yes, it is hereditary, and something we have to watch for, the signs and symptoms.

Since I was tied down at home with my professional job and my full-time job taking care of my husband, I had to direct my support and care for my brother through emotional support, calling often, reassuring him, praying with him. He died after about six years, which is the normal life expectancy. He became an invalid also with loss of memory right at the end.

One of the hardest things in life is losing a sibling. The next hardest thing is losing a sibling mentally. My sister has suffered for many years with Alzheimer's to the point of not knowing her family, her husband, me.

It is very difficult to try to help her emotionally because her memory span is only seconds. She constantly asks, "who are you?" Her husband passed away recently and as far as we know she isn't aware that he is gone. How can anyone help someone in this state? As a caregiver, it is heartbreaking that I can't reach the one I care for so much.

I recently returned home after taking care of my youngest brother who had Parkinson's disease, too! His disease was pretty advanced, but he was still able to live at home and get around on his own.

He fell and was taken to emergency where he was diagnosed with a brain bleed, which led to a stroke. His tongue and throat were paralyzed so he could never eat or drink. This led to a feeding tube. He went to rehab and worked really hard to get well, but with his weakened state he couldn't recover. From the moment he realized he could not get well and go home, I could see him slowly giving up. It was like watching my dad all over again.

I stayed with my brother every day, making sure he got proper medical care, taking care of his personal, spiritual, and emotional needs, telling him constantly that he was loved. After a month with him, he went into organ failure and died in his sleep. I returned home after his funeral and threw myself into planting beautiful flowers, resting, regrouping, (I needed total self-care and recovery). I have been so deeply hurt by losing so many family members that I love, siblings deteriorating before my eyes due to cancer. I've prayed for them and with them to help with their comfort.

My mother died at the age of ninety-two. She was the matriarch of the family and was a devout Christian woman who raised her family by example, teaching us self-worth, honesty, integrity, and love for family and God. She woke our family every morning singing gospel songs in the kitchen while making a huge breakfast. She was my rock and her loss was devastating.

I have admired several people through the years for their endurance through hard times. One of the people I admire the most is a very dear friend who went through several botched surgeries, disfiguration, months of hospitalizations. Yet her frame of mind and determination is a real witness to others on how to overcome all of the hard things that come our way. She is a shining light, encouraging others, reassuring others, making everyone feel special. Telling everyone, "you can do this."

As a registered nurse for thirty years, I've taken care of many patients in critical care units, taking care of their constant needs, providing them comfort and reassurance, as well as comfort to the families. As a critical care unit nurse, I've worked with patients who lost their health permanently, as well as some going through terrible diseases, losing limbs, losing their ability to ever recover to a normal life, losing hope, and even dying. These are just a few of the things we deal with as we work in the healthcare industry.

The professional approach is to be empathetic, not sympathetic, not allowing yourself to become emotionally involved. But, in so many situations, how can you not? How many nights did I clock out and cry all the way home! Too many to count.

On my days off, I planned fun things with friends: dinners, luncheons, working out at the gym, spending many hours in the dance studio preparing for the next national competition, hiking, long walks with my dog, church, and church groups (much needed self-therapy).

I spent over two years in the covid 19 units. It was the hardest thing I have ever done as a professional. Most of these patients were so seriously ill. Their isolation from their families was traumatic because family was not allowed to visit.

In our units, we had iPads available for them to communicate with their loved ones. This was so helpful for the patients and the families. And, in the patient's last days, most of them not conscious, the families could see them and talk to them, telling them they loved them and giving them permission to go.

It is the opinion of many that the only people who died from covid 19 had underlying conditions. This is often the case, but many did not.

I had a twenty-three-year-old patient who presented very, very ill. He was a perfectly healthy young man before getting ill. He only lived for three days. I am sorry to say that he was just one of many, some losing an entire family! There are so many situations that we deal with in the medical field that tear at the very soul of the caregiver. The sorrow of the ones left behind and the staff as well was devastating to everyone. The nurses had to take care of each other.

The family not being able to give their loved one a proper burial or even attend their funeral was so hard for them.

Another thing that caregivers have to consider when our loved one is with us for a long time is that there are times when we feel so tired and drained. We feel tremendous sadness, depression, feelings of being inadequate and useless, feeling trapped, feeling like we can't go on but are still committed to continue. These are real feelings that we go through over time and we must acknowledge them. These are the times when we have someone in place that is willing to step in and give us a break, some time to breathe. To do fun things, take a trip, experience life outside of sickness. We must trust that that person will give the best of care, assuring the loved one that they are safe, secure, and loved. That their needs will be met, and that we will be back.

As caregivers, we must also look at the patient's side of the situation. The sadness they feel, the depression, feeling useless and being in the way. We must help them through these times.

As a widow for fourteen years, I retired recently and moved across the country to be near my family. I don't find retirement to be desirable and it is hard to adjust to not having a real schedule. Leaving all my friends has been hard, too. I am now learning to apply to myself all the things I have learned along the way, to be happy and healthy in my present circumstances. I'm writing my upcoming book, and the opportunity to contribute to this beautiful book. I'm settling in.

My desire is to share some of the many hard times we go through to as caregivers so I can give those who are struggling some insight. It is hard, taxing, and tiring. But, it is rewarding, too, as you see the appreciation on the faces of your patients and the families who struggle through hard times.

Janet Ward

Janet Ward grew up on a farm, the daughter of a farmer. She has three children, several grandchildren and great-grandchildren. Janet has traveled extensively for medical missions as well as for pleasure. Her hobbies include ballroom dancing and writing.

Janet worked for thirty-two years as an RN in the critical setting. She has written prose since 1973 and published her first book in 2017. As she continues to write, she wants to relate life experiences to her audience through the eyes of the average person: Celebrations and disappointments of life, the joy and irony of relationships, and the obvious need that we have for each other.

Connect with Janet at jawilwa@gmail.com.

CHAPTER 10

My Pain Reminded Me of My Destiny

by Kim Robinson

I wondered how this could be. My oldest son's graduation and I'm in some incredible pain, from just sitting for too long. At least it appeared that way to me. I'm trying to race to get to his graduation, to get to the building where he is graduating high school from. I'm trying to run, but only in my mind. Because of the pain, my body is only letting me walk at, what appears to be, a snail's pace. But I was optimistic about making it on time.

Hope is the thing with feathers that perches in the soul and sings the tune without the words, and never stops at all.
~Emily Dickinson

I honestly believe that. My hope in God helped me to make it there just in time to see him walk across the stage.

I will never fail you. I will never abandon you.
Hebrews 13:5

He lifted me out of the pit of despair, out of the mud in the
mire. He set my feet on solid ground and steadied me as I
walked along. Palms 40:2

My condition did not last very long, maybe five or six months. I just did not understand what was going on in my body. All I knew was one day I woke up and did not feel good getting out of the bed. Then, when I would go to the bathroom, to sit on the toilet, it was quite painful. Just sitting for longer than fifteen minutes would actually hurt to get up from where I was sitting.

I was clueless as to what was going on. I went to the doctor and the doctor could not find anything. So my husband suggested to start medicating myself, hoping that that would help me to feel better. I'm not sure it did anything to really help me. Maybe, in my mind, it did.

My next thought was to consider physical therapy. I was thinking that maybe something in me needed movement in the proper way, so I decided to visit a physical therapist in the hopes of relieving some pain. The first thing the physical therapist told me to do was to wean myself off of all the medicine. I practiced some physical therapy, but I really wasn't seeing a lot happen till I decided to do some other things a bit differently.

I noticed that when I was younger, in my twenties, that I used to exercise quite a bit. In fact, I love exercising. I enjoy it so much that I used to teach aerobics when I was in the United States Navy. I did that for about a year, and I had a ball! But, as life progressed and I had children, I left exercise and me on the back burner. So here I am in my forties and in pain and not understanding what in the world is going on. So I decided, you know what? I need to pray. I prayed for God to help me figure this thing out and heal me. Also, I felt like God was talking to me about my lifestyle.

My lifestyle had changed over the years. I really wasn't looking at the food I was putting in my body. I wasn't looking at what I was doing as far as movement and exercise, the biggest being movement. Helping my kids do something or going to the grocery store was what I mainly did for exercise. I needed more movement in my life. That's what I figured. I said, "You know what? Let me try this. Let me try to start exercising, walking, moving, and truly doing it consistently." Also, I decided that I needed to change my diet and start eating better foods. It was time to really look at what I'm eating. So I did just that.

You know what? I noticed changes. I noticed from the exercise, from the physical therapy and from the eating that I was changing. As time went on, the pain went away. Oh, what a glorious thing that was. What a glorious day that was for me, really. It was a gradual thing. I noticed that the pain was getting less and less and then one day, it happened. The pain was gone. That is what motivated me to really speak to others about their health and movement in their lives and so concerning that thought, I said, "You know what? I think I should consider being a health coach." That way I could talk to other people and also discover great information on how to really speak to my life and to other people's lives to reach them on a higher level in a way that I could never do so otherwise. Then I went to school to become a Health Coach. A year after my training, I ran into a good friend that I went to Bible study with. She told me about some products that she was using that were concentrated plant based food. What do we need? We all need plant-based foods and much more than we naturally eat. So I tried it out and I was like, wow, this is good. After a while, I noticed the difference. I felt a consistent elevated amount of energy in my body. I told myself, "You know what, I'm going start telling other people about this."

Soon, my kids were taking it and I felt like they were feeling better, and we definitely had less doctor visits. Then, I started thinking about movement. I was thinking, wow, I love movement. I love dancing. Why am I not doing this with people, groups of people? What about personal training group exercise? I mean, I did it in the military because the aerobics exercise instructor was leaving and he needed someone to take it over. But now? I was just like, huh? I could actually do this, and so I decided to go back to school, and become a personal trainer.

I'm so glad that I now get the opportunity to speak into people's lives like never before. I get to help them with movement. I get to help them with nutrition.

I have even started helping them with their overall mindset. I had noticed that for a lot of my clients it's really a mindset thing. It's not so much that they can't lose weight. They may say that they can't eat right and they can't move their body. That's what they say. But that's not really the way it is. It's so great having an opportunity to work with people and to speak with them and speak truth into what they get to be in their lives. They get to be everything that they desire to be, and that's what I love about what I do. I feel like I get to take myself along with them to the next level. This is such a wonderful thing. When I think about it, I think about all of the people that have come into my life and have helped me to get to my next level. I feel like this is just another way of me being able to give back to all the good that I have been given. Their future is bright and filled with a great living hope that should never fail. Their hope should be a light. Light arises in the darkness. For the upright, He is gracious and compassionate and righteous. We get to use what we get in our lives.

I love sharing the truth about what it has taken for me to feel better. I love to speak the truth to others. That's where I get my joy. My joy is in being used to help bring out the best in others. It is simply reminding people of who they are and helping them to increase their faith in what they can do and who they can be. What I love so much about my clients is I get to hear their truths. Some may say to me, "Well, I don't mind working out a little bit, but I want to be able to eat whatever I want." Others may say, "Well, I can watch what I eat, but I really do not want to work out. I do not want to do any exercising." So, here's the balance. We get the ones that don't want to eat right to want to eat right, and the ones that don't like to exercise to find something that they love doing that can move their body, right? I feel that mindset is everything. It is the catalyst that allows you to truly be able to go from one level to the next in life.

When I think about mindset, I think a lot about the way I was when I was in the military. Those were some great days for me and quite a few changes in my life. It was a time of experiencing a lot of new things, at one time. I joined the military in 1986 and it was a time that we were at peace here in the United States. I signed up for the military, hoping to be able to get some money for college, and that happened. I took a few classes, but I really did not make the most of my time through taking classes. I did, however, make the most of my adventure of being in the United States Navy.

I started off in Winter Harbor, Maine. For two years I faced the cold and what I considered to be some of the worse snowstorms of my life. I was living in the Acadia National Park area, which is so beautiful. This beautiful rock climber's dream is a tourist area that's right outside of where the military base was. There I learned the importance of learning your job and getting your tasks done in a timely manner. Of course, we all were fit because we had physical fitness training tests that we were scheduled to take twice a year. We knew we had to exercise. We had to keep ourselves in shape and most of us were pretty young anyway, so we were pretty good to go. We had to meet a certain standard just to get in.

I believe that my military time really helped me to shape my life and teach me how to go out and get those things that may not always be easy to get. One experience that I had in the military was in basic training where I was warned by my recruiter that I would have to take a swim test. I did not know how to swim, but she told me not to worry and reassured me that I would be taught to swim. That is, sort of, what they did. The training was quite an experience. We took about an hour to learn how to do the back float, and those who still couldn't do it or were afraid to do it, had to come back for swimming lessons. The only issue with that is if we had to come back for swimming lessons, we had to go to swim class on your own and anytime you went anywhere on your own, you had to go double time, which means you had to run to wherever you went if you were not with your Basic Training group in the military. I considered my sense of direction, or lack of it, and concluded that I would be running for days, trying to find the building.

So, I decided that today is the day that I get to swim. That was my mindset. After I learned how to do the backstroke, I was then given an opportunity to jump into the water from the diving board. From the diving board we were supposed to slightly jump up and leap in. Once we did that, we arose up out of the water on our backs and we performed a back float across the pool. I dove in and I felt like I was diving forever, the endless dive it was. As time went on, and I began to lean back to float, the instructors said, "Yes, you can, you're doing it." I was actually doing it! Before I knew it, they were telling me that I was halfway across the pool and I was rejoicing in my mind, but still concerned about getting the rest of the way across the pool. Finally,

I completed my float session. As I got out of the pool, my company commander spoke to me. She looked at me and said, "Huh, I can't do it, huh?" But I could tell that she was proud that I had successfully completed it. So was I.

Basic training was not so bad for me. I didn't really do a whole lot of terrible things like some other ladies in my company had to do. Some of us had to work in the mess hall aka the kitchen. They worked crazy hours in the kitchen from morning to night. I don't think prisoners work as hard as they worked that week. They would get out at about 8:00 o'clock at night and get up about 4:00 o'clock in the morning to work. I thank God for my recruiter. She had given me the lowdown on that issue. She told me to make sure that I volunteered for the band or choir and to make sure I did not work in the mess hall because they would be up late.

I had a week of bliss in my dorm room because all I had to do was go to choir that week while a lot of the other ladies were going to the mess hall and working numerous hours. I thank Miss Barbara Parker, my recruiter, for that. I served in the military for four years. My last year was the year that I truly was introduced to fitness, the awesomeness of exercise, and being able to work as an exercise instructor. My sponsor was selected to show me around the base when I came to my last duty station in Diego Garcia. She took me everywhere she went and introduced me to her friends and associates and simply helped me to become a part of the new life that I now had. As time progressed, she wanted to go to the gym. When she took me to the gym, she said to me, "Hey, do you like to exercise, because this guy is pretty good?" I said, "Yes, I love to exercise." "We can exercise in the back," she said. "We'll stay in the back because he's pretty good and he's kind of hard to keep up with." I had a ball and was able to keep up with his pace the whole time. Once he finished teaching the class, he approached me and said, "Wow, you stayed with me the entire workout and this was your first time. You're pretty good at this." I told him that I like movement and dance. He told me, "You know what, I'm going to be leaving in a few months, and we're going to need some new instructors. Is this something that you might happen to consider?" I was like, ah, no, not really. I was just having fun. And he said, "Well, we're going to need people and I don't mind training you. I will set up your music for you as well. I can do that for you." I replied, "Huh. I guess I'll think about it."

A few weeks later, I told him, yes. I have loved exercise, helping people exercise ever since then. I took a little time off when I was having babies and staying busy at work. There were some other life choices that I decided to take on. I had done no training in group exercise for quite a while. A few years ago, I was like, you know what, I need to get back into exercising. I get the chance to take other people to the next level. Their fitness routine in their lives is changed. Some people will live longer because they've decided to put movement back in their lives. They'll live longer because they decided to change their eating habits. They'll live longer because they've changed their mindset on who they are. They will be reminded of who they can be. Oh, how I love my job. God, our God will take care of the hidden things, but the revealed things are our business. Deuteronomy 20:29

In life, God does reveal things to us, and when he does, we need to take advantage of those insights. Because of the things that God has revealed to me regarding who I am, I like to pass that on to others. They get to know who they are as well. This is such a wonderful thing about life and really just us being human beings on this earth. We are all here to help each other in some way. That's what some of us get to discover in our lives. Our lives are a constant journey. We're on a journey every day. No one knows really what's going to happen from one day to the next. We get to use the day we're in, the time we're in, to be the best.

We get to do what we know that we are called to do. Those things that we feel deep down inside our gut that we're supposed to do. That's how we can have a life that is filled with joy. There is sorrow, yes, but through the sorrow, you come back up with peace. Not always knowing that you can get through the valleys, through the rivers, through life, by knowing who you are, by trusting in God. With God, all things are possible, to those that believe. So, believe so you can receive.

Kim Robinson

Kim Robinson is a Certified Health Coach, who is Certified in Hormone Health and Personal Training. She loves showing others what she has done to help them to achieve their health and wellness goals. She is married to Larry Robinson and has two bonus sons, Jason and Larry Jr., five other boys, Austin, Tyler, Wesley, Vincent and Ethan, and one daughter, Lydia.

Kim boasts that all she has been able to do in her life, for family and others, is due to having the Lord God directly working in her life to lead and guide her footsteps and gives Him the honor and praise for everything that she does and has been given.

Connect with Kim at http://mywellnessmatters.life.

CHAPTER 11

Lessons I Had to Learn to Begin Healing Myself

*From the Diary of a Certified Hypnotherapist
and Provoker of Possibility*

by Lauren Best

Before 2020, the act of healing didn't mean much more to me than a goosebump, scrape combo that eventually would leave me with a small scar and a new landscape on my shin. The idea of healing something that I couldn't see, that wasn't physical, really wasn't something that I had ever thought very much of within my own reality or had ever considered would be a part of my story. Here I am, two-plus years after I began my journey of self-healing with a new level of confidence, a deep trust in my intuition, and a certification in Hypnotherapy. The last of that list was the most unexpected—who would have thought? I sure didn't.

Just like the majority of the world, I had been conditioned to chase external recognition and achievement based on societal norms. All the while working towards discovering the next best thing. Like many other perfectionists who are stuck in survival mode, operating with a nervous system on its last nerve, I too, had to have the wind knocked out of me before I really even considered making any change.

I wish this was a story of recognizing that I had so much self-worth that I knew right away that the workplace I was in was toxic enough that I could give myself permission to walk out the door. That my relationships didn't have to exist with unconditional love or that my health and my happiness were worth taking a pause for. That it was even an option to simply give myself the space to rest, to recalibrate and turn inward to figure out what I truly wanted in my life, without having to have my next move all planned out.

Instead, an undeniable voice inside my head kept telling me I should stick it out to finish what I started until I had another sure thing lined up. And that having compassion for another human meant that I had to sacrifice my values and compassion toward myself. That my body had to begin shutting down, breaking out in hives, and having my appendix rupture before I would actually begin to seriously listen to it. What happened next is where the story really starts.

When I look back on the beginning of 2020, there were so many clear catalysts to the downfall of everything I knew about my life. And those same catalysts were what helped me to discover what was actually important to me and whom I needed to become to live my life on my own terms. Depends on how you look at it.

At the time, I just didn't really get that yet. It truly had to take multiple wild things and a series of events for me to end up back in Canada, the home country that I hadn't called home for nearly 7 years, for me to be forced to figure out what I was going to do with my life. The reality then was that I still didn't get that this is what the universe needed me to do. The universe needed me to be stopped completely in my tracks, because of the choices I had made, to be operating in my life out of such severe misalignment.

I realize now that not every molehill is disguised as a mountain or that all things that feel important to you are worth fighting for. If you explained it to me like that at the time, I don't think I would have dismissed the truth of that understanding. Rather, I was just too stuck operating in survival mode and overdrive that I don't think the discombobulation of my nervous system would have been able to receive or process this sentiment.

We'd need an entire novel for me to fill in the blanks of all of the things and experiences I went through to get to where I am today. So instead, I want to share with you some of the biggest lessons that have become monumental healing ingredients thus far in my life. Most of the time what we really need to do is just pause to reflect on the instrumental moments in our lives. Those that have shown us the proof that we can heal ourselves and that we can grow. Because of how far these lessons have taken me, I will continue to prioritize these experiences, these rituals, these realizations as long as I shall live.

Lesson 1: You Can Find the Right People to Support You as You Heal

When you read this, if you were mentally and emotionally where I was back in 2020, one of the most important things I'll tell you is that I didn't get to the place I'm at now, in January 2023, on my own. Yes, it was important for me to reconnect to my intuition and turn inward to rediscover the deep answers inside of myself, but it was also through the wisdom and support of some amazingly powerful and compassionate woman that I found my way back to myself.

You see, most of the time we can know all of the right answers on paper, and we can be given a list of all the tools or habits we can implement to find self-love, gratitude, forgiveness and growth, but when there has been so much piled up on top of you, just simply finding your guides, mentors, and soul-friends can be a great place to start.

If you're like me, seeing a list of affirmations or hot tips on social media can feel inspiring for a second, but without a container or a space of guidance it is really unlikely that I will get started on integrating a practice on my own terms—it's more likely that you'll find me in front of the tv watching some unrealistic reality show. So it has been instrumental for me to seek out communities, people and spaces where I will be asked introspective questions and where I will feel supported and understood.

I accepted invitations from friends to connect me with their networks of other amazing human beings. I attended workshops and webinars that would teach me about concepts that opened my mind. I became serious about recognizing my own patterns and how these patterns were impacting my life. I found the right coaches, mentors, readers and peers that really opened my world to see new possibilities for my life beyond my current reality. One of which changed my life profoundly was hypnosis.

If it weren't for seeking out this support, my life would look really different right now. Today, I still spend lots of time watching reality tv, but now I also prioritize showing up at different community events and scheduling my monthly hypnosis and mentorship sessions. On the other end of it, I am helping other people through their own journeys of transformation by creating spaces of opportunity, collaboration, visualization, connection, and self-discovery.

I credit my experience of connecting to all of the incredible women that have become so instrumental in my healing journey for this reminder: *It is important for me to trust the impact of putting myself in places and spaces with people that are energetically aligned to me at whatever point in time I really need their guidance.*

Lesson 2: It's Important to Start Being Honest with Yourself

I find myself struggling to figure out how to even start talking about this lesson. If I was brutally honest with myself, I would have come up with the sharp, quick, witty opening sentence that I think I should have. Maybe not.

Getting honest with yourself starts with checking in to really notice where you are showing up authentically, or not, in your life. You see, there is a difference between showing up wholeheartedly in the ways that feel good and that match your values or showing up in the ways we think we should, because of societal norms, conditioning, or self-imposed expectations that no one else really cares about.

I had to learn that in order to interrupt the patterns that were keeping me from showing up authentically, I had to introduce a new level of self-awareness. This is another place where introspection and self-coaching have been key for me. I had to get real and ask myself if I was truly being honest with myself or not. *Where was I living inauthentically? What do I like? What do I not like? What is my gut telling me? What makes me feel uncomfortable or good in my body?*

As of late, there have been many moments in designing my own business, where I have been taking action out of fear instead of by listening to my gut. I was creating offers that weren't aligned with how I could best use my energy and make an impact. I was limiting myself to a specific audience, because I had learned that niching down and speaking to one type of person is how you'll be successful. Yet the evidence showed me, repeatedly, that this wasn't true for me. Sometimes our patterns can be too comfortable and without that space to pause and ask the tough questions, we can find ourselves stuck in a loop that doesn't allow us to operate from full authenticity and potential.

It took me a long time to realize that it is healthy to recognize our patterns and outgrow them. That if I simply showed up as my most authentic and honest me, I would stop attracting people, energy, and opportunities that were misaligned. *What if I could simply attract the people, situations, places and spaces, opportunities and experiences that were right for me, just by being me?*

Still to this day, I struggle with finding the balance between offering myself compassion and holding myself accountable. Perhaps bringing more weight to one or the other is necessary at times. I've concluded that it would be extremely difficult for me to design an honest and authentic life without just being me.

For me, this really involves going beyond the level of self-awareness to grounding myself with different tools and rituals. I have explored how I can use mindfulness to romanticize my life and notice what I find beauty in, how my human design chart can guide me through understanding more about myself, and how journaling can be my super tool for getting out and inside of my head. Perhaps these can work for you, too, but you won't know until you try.

When we get serious about creating change and being honest with ourselves it can feel scary, because we risk letting go of everything that we've ever known. We risk letting go of people that aren't able to understand who we'll grow into. We risk not recognizing ourselves anymore. In my opinion, the transformation that is possible is one hundred times over worth the risk.

Lesson 3: Look for the Signs Where Something Inside of You is Telling You to Do Things Differently

Parallel to the act of healing, working with my subconscious mind definitely was another thing that didn't mean much of anything to me before 2021. I had a very basic understanding of emotional intelligence, spirituality, and the power of visualization.

I had seen my mom practice years of Kundalini Yoga and witnessed how much of an impact that practice had on how she centered herself and her emotions. She had invited me to try it on different occasions, one of which I remember as this really light and happy experience, another as an experience where I felt so consumed by other people's auras that I went running for the hills. She had also taken me to many meditation workshops. At the time, I didn't really appreciate meditation as an instrumental tool that I could use in my daily life for finding that same neutrality that I now try to sit with as much as possible.

I remember wondering if I was even meditating, because my mind was still in overdrive and I only felt comfortable doing it lying down, while the rest of the class sat propped up on their fancy meditation cushions. I did consider making an effort to sign up for regular classes and then I never did. Like I said before, without the right space and places to show up for these practices, I have always really struggled to prioritize even the things that I wanted to do even though I knew they could be life-changing. In my case, the undervaluing of what these experiences could potentially bring me had more to do with just being too young and not fully understanding or connecting the dots to the bigger picture. I was busy doing my own thing.

On the other side, as I reflect on my behaviors provoked by these experiences, I notice the little rebel inside of me rearing its curious head and influencing me to just do what felt good. I notice the glimpses of me instinctively making a decision to do things my way and to also trust that something might not be what I need at that moment in time. You could call it lazy, but I can call it intuition and authenticity. Rebellion doesn't have to be loud or look disruptive, it can also be simple and quiet.

Lesson 4: Learning to Trust That Uncertainty May Always Be There to Carry You to Where You're Meant to Go

When I moved back to my childhood home with my family in August of 2020, I brought with me massive energetic and emotional piles as a result of the most intense experiences from the seven months prior. The piles were made up of shock, grief, confusion, fear, and stress to name a few. I returned without a job or direction in sight. I had never imagined myself moving back to Canada, at least not without some sort of inspirational plan that would have been on my own terms.

The uncertainty of how long I was going to be here, where I was going to live next, what type of job I would have, and how long the pandemic would last were some of the biggest wonders on my mind. Guess what, these same uncertainties still exist in my current reality. What's changed is that the fear of the unknown isn't as suffocating as it was back then.

Even though I have grown a million miles from the place I was then to where I am now, I am still a stay-at-home-child. I have no idea where I am going to live next. I have no idea what my work could look like a month from now. The pandemic is still going on. Instead, the uncertainty that I am experiencing now looks like appreciation for the privilege I have to spend so much more time with my parents than I had ever imagined under their roof. Having the freedom of travelling to different places in the globe in my new nomadic life. Getting to be in control of the projects and people I work with as I continue to grow and explore new ways of working. And I am now prioritizing my health beyond productivity or doing things I think I have to do—no more FOMO.

With embracing uncertainty comes the ability to truly and deeply trust in the timing of my life. It has been a huge, huge struggle to get to this place of trust, and I know it's something I will continue to work on for the rest of my life. I know it's something that I can help other people find more comfort in too.

Using hypnosis to rewrite a lot of my old stories and limiting beliefs and facing my fears head-on have been instrumental in this. Taking time to move my body by going for walks and practicing Qi Gong reminds me to slow down. Letting go of the pressure to have a perfect plan in my business has released my need to control all of the moving pieces that typically put me in burnout. Having clarity in my values, my mission, and my vision is what grounds me.

Lesson 5: Healing is Not a Destination, But a Lifelong Experience

Of all of the lessons I've learned on this journey of healing, the most important has been to not be fooled by the idea that healing is a destination. Instead, the journey of healing can become a lifelong process of continuously levelling up, if you want it to. Only if you continue to be open to this idea that you can keep receiving more, keep shedding more, keep growing into newer versions of yourself, that your standards can change, that you can reevaluate your boundaries, and reinvent yourself time and time again, will you see how this journey of healing can keep showing up for you.

This is how you will see that healing can appear in every version of our reality. What changes over time is the tools that we carry and implement when we need them. It's the amount of space we have to hold discomfort, the new levels of resilience that we build as we experience more, how quickly we transmute our emotions to find neutral energy, the compassion and self-care that we gift ourselves, and the self-awareness and openness that we need to continuously grow and let go of the things that no longer need to live with us.

Lesson 6: Be Your Own Provoker of Possibility

As time goes on we can find more clarity on what it is we want or desire, or what we no longer stand for or want to put up with. Without leaving that space to receive the right support, to become honest with ourselves, to listen to our inner voice when it is guiding us to do things our own way, to trust in the uncertainty, and to be open to new experiences, we can unknowingly shut ourselves off from chance.

And as you experience new possibilities in your life, you may begin to notice that the environment in which you experience them will shift and that you too will also shift. Without even trying too hard at all, you can begin experiencing the opening of new doors to new possibilities, that you hadn't even imagined possible.

Lauren Best

Lauren Best is a Certified Hypnotherapist and Provoker of Possibility, who works with Curious Individuals, Creative Entrepreneurs, and Conscious Companies who are ready to explore how they can do things differently in their work and life. With the teaching of various tools, she inspires others to dive into a world of self-discovery and growth where they can unlock an even greater potential inside of themselves using their subconscious minds.

Her superpower is helping people explore new possibilities for living a life they love by guiding them back to themselves, helping them reconnect and trust in their intuition and building confidence like they've never experienced before. She creates spaces of support and collaboration to help these folks move through the noise, envision and come up with new ideas, and create bite-sized plans of action that supports their desired area of transformation.

Lauren has collaborated with public and private sector organizations, small businesses and solopreneurs across the globe from Canada to the UK, Netherlands, Australia, The United States and Singapore

Connect with Lauren at https://lauren-best.com.

CHAPTER 12

Angels Amongst Us

by Lindsey Hagood

I believe there are angels amongst us. Sent down to us from somewhere up above. They come to you and me in our darkest hour. To show us how to live. To teach us how to give. To guide us with a light of love. ~Helen Keller

---

I remember growing up as a child seeing visions of angels, the kind you see dancing in the moonlight or floating above in the sky. They had white wispy wings that expanded out about four feet in length on each side. There were short, winged cherubs, too. I had quite an imagination and they looked like cherubs you see in magazines or books.

I could feel their spirits all around me. While growing up, I was always fascinated with their ornate detail. Halloween one year while in grade school, I was an angel. Mom made and sewed for me my adorable white satin robe and gave me a nice shining silver halo adorned with wings of white feathers. Their angelic presence gave me an overwhelming feeling of perfect love; a safe place to cushion the falls of life; a safe place that felt like home.

It brings a smile to my face as I reflect on memories of yesterday's past. I remember standing in line in my angel costume next to a blonde-haired boy I had a crush on. I always felt this shining light within me. It was as if a guided spirit, an angel, was all around me. As a child, it helped navigating through this tough world. I always felt the presence of them guiding me, by my side, protecting me from harm.

Believers, look up – take courage. The angels are nearer than you think. ~Billy Graham

---

Angels come to us in different ways, shapes, and forms. I believe it to be close to what we've read about or studied. I always had this fascinating imaginative relationship with these figurines, as if they were a life source. I came to realize the powerful presence of these magical creatures during my childhood and throughout the course of my adult life.

Angel figurines are the kind you'd see in displays in the Hallmark shop or in the movies. Some are small with chubby cheeks, and then there are those in human form that resemble real life people. They had angel wings that expanded two to four feet wide and were dressed in white robes, of course. It was more like a draped sheet, as their robes are different than the ones I had seen in pictures of God.

At The Art Institute of Houston, where I studied interior design and commercial design, I learned the different periods of art, especially Michelangelo. I had an opportunity to study them, the enormity of them on murals and sky walls, paintings, and the time period where they were very popular.

I loved them so much that my parents started gifting me little angel statues as I grew up. I received them every birthday or holiday and even friends joined in. The gifts were crystal statues, clay collection statues, and more. I realized my connection to them as others saw these figurines in me. I think, perhaps, I was an angel in their eyes, and it was a humbling experience to be compared to an angel, but I didn't think I was one.

I recall a time I dated a boyfriend and he and his friend gave me a bumper sticker that said good girls go to heaven and bad girls go everywhere. I always associated angels with good people and bad people with the devil and was drawn to the more chubby cheeked angelic angels. Due to my fascination with angels and their angelic presence, it was no surprise they would visit me during two different life experiences.

The first time I experienced a real connection with an angel was when I was eighteen. I traveled to Puerto Rico and while visiting a friend I became terribly ill. It was at that time that I floated above my body and traveled to the next room. When I was above the desk, I realized I was flying. I felt the presence of a guardian angel by my side as I went in and out of consciousness. It was just like you've probably heard. I was zooming through time. There were puffy clouds and it was a dream-like setting, yet dark as the light passed through the clouds of smoke. It was eerily quiet, too, as spirits passed by. I knew they were people. They resembled people with hair and full-grown bodies dressed in white gowns. Everything was hazy, so there was not a clear vision of color; just white and gray. I felt as if I were passing through tunnels and then on fast-moving escalators as they zipped on by. White and gray is what I recall and yet it was also a feeling of peace. Everyone had a designated mission as if they were off to their next great assignment.

For he will put his angels in charge of you and guard you in all his ways. ~Psalm 91:11

Throughout the years, I've been blessed to meet many guided and gifted angels. More recently, I had an incredible connection with a healing angel that guided me during a second illness that left me gravely ill.

It was in 2017. I had surgery to remove and replace breast implants. I didn't exactly want the replacements, but the doctor told me I wouldn't be happy otherwise. It was a moment in time where everything stopped and I had this feeling something was wrong.

When I came out of surgery, I was gravely ill and fought infection for three weeks before having an emergency surgery. I saw angels that day. There were three doctors at the end of my bed. Two were together. They had beautiful green eyes and golden tan skin. They were my team to save my life. On my right side was a taller man with curly hair wearing a different kind of robe. His robe was rolled over at the neckline and he had the most amazing blue green ocean eyes I've ever seen. The other two doctors were sharing with me what was going on, that they were there to do emergency surgery and be my team so I could go back to my original surgeon. I immediately opened my eyes, shaking my head and whispered, "no." The other doctor draped in the special white robe whispered, "It's contamination, Lindsey." I remember it like it happened yesterday. I opened my eyes and cried, tears streaming down my face, gasping for air. As I looked back at the other two doctors to my right, I lifted my hand and rolled my finger and whispered, "Let's go."

The golden tan skinned doctor with blue eyes the color of the Caribbean Sea came out of surgery and pulled off his cap. He spoke to my girlfriend (whom I hadn't seen in eight months). She had called me while I was being transported by ambulance to UMC Trauma Center in Las Vegas. He said, "Your girlfriend is very lucky, as a few more hours and I am not sure the outcome would be the same." She will be here for a week and will need to follow up with the medical team. There's a lot of us here, so she's in good care. We believe we got it all and have sent the implants to the lab for testing and pathogens.

As I write this, the moment is surreal, as if everything transpiring back in time. I can feel the moment, see the moment with every ounce of my being. It was the most painful experience I've ever had, yet also the most prolifically inspiring. How can that be, you may ask? As I do often, I just surrendered in that moment to God.

I felt a strong presence around me as I surrendered to an army of angels. I couldn't see them as physical people, but I could feel their spirit. There was a movement of air blowing past me as they gathered around my bed. I could hear them; the noise was so loud. There were thousands of voices in the room all around me. They didn't speak; they made noise as they were gathering, huddling around me and breathing the breath of life into me was what I could hear and feel.

I bow down to pray,
Lord make the worst seem better.
Lord, show me the way.
~Lady Gaga

131

As I came out of surgery, I was wheeled to my room and I remember seeing my girlfriend and her daughter. They brought me a balloon and a little stuffed animal to get well. She said, "Lindsey, that was a close one. I'm going to be here every day for you." I remember tears flowing down my face whispering, "Thank you. Thank you."

A beautiful song with incredible words kept inspiring me during that time. I would just close my eyes, dream of the beach, and sing this song, "I bow down to pray. Lord, make the worst seem better." It's a song I've never heard, yet I could hear it. It helped pass the time until my family arrived and could get to me. They were flying in from Houston, and it was quite a process to get my mother to me. She was petrified to fly since her and daddy's bad trip many years ago that had a bomb on the plane. My oldest niece would accompany her here. I just remembered somehow making a call to have a driver come to get them. They arrived in style, that's for sure, as my niece just went on and on about the driver picking them up, wheeling Meme through the airport and whisking her away in the wheelchair.

It was in that moment of resting, in and out of sleep, that there were angels all around me. This time it was my family and relatives. They were way up high, to the right of my bed, dancing and bobbing up and down in the clouds. Granddaddy was there with his Navy hat on (he flew with the Blue Angels and had just passed). Champ Cooke, a dear friend of my father's who had passed, was there, and Daddy was there. He wasn't wearing his glasses. Grandmother Pat was there, my Meme, her hair all coiffed and dolled up. She looked just like I had remembered. Aunt Hope was there with her beautiful long blonde hair and my great grandmother. She had a scarf wrapped around her neck just like I recalled. It took me a while to figure out who she was, but then I remembered.

The bright light was so bright. I kept reaching into the air to block it away. The light was as bright as the sun and the nurse touched my wrist to bring it down back to my chest. I remember a lot of equipment over to the right of me and I finally said, "What's taking so long? What are you doing? I'm not going to make it." The doctor appeared in the dark of the night and said, "Lindsey, we are on the eighth antibiotic." I just remember crying and saying, "I'm not going to make it. Get my mother here."

When the noise settled down from the doctors and nurses over me, I reached back up to the sky, the sun, a bright ball of white light, electrifying energy like the sun. It was healing. I wanted it; I reached for it. The noises to my left were so loud. I told the nurses to tell them to leave. There was no one there, they said. They were there. There must have been thousands of them gathered.

As I continued resting, I could feel them doing work, praying over me. It was a calmness I'd never felt. I looked up again and felt a tall man at the end of the bed. He was so tall. He was the one in the surgery room. I rested assured knowing he was doing his work and I would be just fine.

Wherever you go and whatever you do, may you
have a guardian angel over you. ~unknown

Going home, I still struggled with illness, followed by another emergency surgery. This time they found twenty-six pathogens and one was unknown. Again, I relied on my faith and fitness goals to help me withstand this storm. My health was very uncertain, and I had a difficult time overcoming my health battle.

I was blessed to have a friend to reach out through social media and give me a name of a healing faith angel. Her name was Lacey and I made arrangements to connect with her long distance. I was now in Florida, healing near the beach. We started long distance healing sessions and I connected with her immediately. Upon arriving back in Las Vegas, I met up with her in person. Together we worked wonders through releasing trauma and poisons throughout my body. She cleared my chakras and I remember it took a good five sessions before really connecting and releasing myself to her work. It was at that time that I felt the presence of my angel relatives and I knew I, too, was an angel. That I could utilize the spirits of good for my healing and be so blessed by this angel that helped to heal me.

Lacey worked feverishly getting to the source inside and I remember just crying, releasing the pain within. I could feel the pain within and see where the infection was inside my chest.

Nevertheless, the goal was to release the toxic energy there or the subconscious fear of relentless pain. So, I did. I felt a huge shift and screamed. I cried so hard. I knew that it was done and over. It had released itself and I was gifted with this incredible being and release of the anguish inside of me.

Discovering this gift of angels amongst us empowered me. I knew I could be healed with the help of angels, God, and I could heal myself. I've learned we walk by faith and not by sight; even the biblical passage that states this is so powerful and true.

Faith is believing in things you cannot see
but believe in your heart. ~Hebrews 11:1 (NCV)

Angels are amongst us in our darkest hours. We may not believe it, but I can share with you that they are real and they do exist. Many are family relatives that have passed and friends we've met along the way. They are even you and me. We just have to believe.

Lindsey Hagood

Lindsey Hagood is an Entrepreneur, Fitness and Health advocate, Certified Life Coach, Former Model, and Motivational Speaker on a mission to inspire others from illness to wellness through Living an Inspired Life.

She is 11x certified in the fitness and health industry, loves life with all her heart, and thanks God, her family, and many friends for prayers on her recovery. Her suffering has not been for nothing.

Her message of Live Inspired! Through Faith and Fitness comes from her belief of being passionate about her belief in God and being physically fit through wellness for life.

Since Lindsey's grave illness following surgery in 2017 and a 28-month Recovery, she has gone on to place Top 10 in the World at the WBFF Bahamas show in 35+ division Bikini & Fitness, Transformation Model, and her most rewarding gift of helping others with her Fitness Health Coaching App.

2022 has been rewarding, as she has been featured in "The Travel Wins" podcast sharing her story from illness with implant poisoning,

Dr. Lycka's podcast "How to Live a Fantastic Life," "Live Through Your Brand" with Lynne and Will, and featured Co-Author in *bLU – Business, Life, and the Universe vol. 6* – International Bestseller.

Lindsey's greatest achievement is that of inspiring others. She dedicates this to her family, many friends across the world, and those overcoming illness to wellness!

Connect with Lindsey at https://linktr.ee/lindseyhagood.

CHAPTER 13

Honoring My Gifts

by Maria Elena De Lira

Growing up in Mexico in a rural area surrounded by nature, I was always running around looking for things to discover like poking bugs out of the ground to see what lived beneath my bare feet. During the evenings I would climb onto the roof and daydream of faraway places to explore while looking at the sparkly lights on the horizon wondering what could be over there!

The bright lights turned out to be in the United States, and my dream of being up close to those lights came true when one day when a relative gave me the opportunity to go. I wanted to see the sparkly lights for myself and with so much determination inside, I knew I would do whatever I could to see it for myself; my relative told me in order to cross into the USA I needed papers. As a child full of innocence, I quickly started searching for papers off the ground and when I gave them the bundle of papers they laughed at my attempt. "No, not those types of papers, you do not have them here." Being so young, I could not understand the legalities of such paperwork then, so even in my disappointment, I kept dreaming of those sparkly lights just calling my name! Several months had then passed and my relatives from the USA made it a reality for me to see all those lights!

Raymondville, Texas, was just a rural town and there weren't that many lights to see back in the '70s. However, I was taken to see lots of sparkly lights somewhere within the city. I was loving that I was able to see so clearly in the night under the lights, something I was never able to do in Mexico. I danced and jumped all over the place; I was so happy because finally my wish came true! The feeling in my chest of so much joy and hope lasted for several days, it was an experience I could not forget. It felt like my little heart was bursting at the seams! Weeks passed with me living with my aunt, and many times she had to tell me to not make noise since I was a child out of school and someone could call the cops so it would be better to stay inside. I grew restless after a while, and I asked them to take me back to Mexico where I could actually run wild and free and be with my family again. When they did, I was so happy to be back home.

I loved visiting my grandparents. There was always things to do and enjoy which went well for the restless spirit I had inside. Me and my cousins would take off walking through the corn fields whenever we felt like going, and we knew that we were going to spend the night since it was far. We didn't care, though, because we loved visiting them. My grandmother always had chores for us to do whenever we went to visit and when she heard us coming, she would start taking out the dirty dishes and other items that needed cleaning.

There would also be a line of people on specific days waiting outside to be seen by my grandma, who was the medicine woman in the region. I loved when she would send me to gather herbs and plants from her garden! The smell of all the plants was exhilarating. Mother Nature had a way to fill my soul with its senses and I would dance and laugh and run in the garden full of glee like I did that day seeing those lights in Raymondville. I felt so privileged just to be allowed to go in there as it was my grandma's sacred space. We knew the plants were meant to heal some ailment and grandma would prepare healing poultices and different remedies for each individual depending on their specific needs or pains.

She was also the midwife; her hands were the first ones to hold me when I was born. Everyone knew who she was, since she basically attended every birth in the area and sometimes she would go and check on all the new mothers while riding her donkey. Some days, we were blessed to ride with her where people would come up and give her fruits, meat, eggs, and even chickens as payment for her services. She was always bartering with people when they didn't have money to pay.

My grandfather was a beautiful human being. Whenever we stayed the night, he would wake us up and take us to go milk the cows. We would line up and he would milk the cow's milk straight into our cups. Oh, man! Each sip was so delicious! We would try and line up several times to get more milk in our little stomachs waiting with milk mustaches on our faces. We also knew that milk was another source of income for my grandparents, and we were very blessed to have free access to this.

Grandpa loved being a grandpa. He would play with all his grandkids and would line us up around him where he would get on our level just like a kid himself. He would then tickle us with his beard on our faces, tickle us with his toes on our tummies. He was in heaven hearing us all laughing, and we enjoyed spending time with him and his beautiful soul. He had many things to do on the ranch; take cows to the pasture, cut cactus to feed them, take care of the mother cows, and even delivering the babies. He would also take charge of harvesting the fields.

My father had a drinking problem, but I don't remember seeing my grandpa drink. On one occasion, my father came home drunk and started arguing with my mother and I saw him hit her. I was five years old at the time. I was afraid for my mom, so I got up and launched myself at him defending my mom. He threw me against the wall and I landed on the floor unconscious. I don't know how long I lay there. My siblings didn't get involved. The physical abuse went on for several years. I didn't know that the family was going through financial trouble. The drinking wasn't helping the financial situation either.

My father decided to move us to the city when I was nine years old and things drastically changed. On the ranch, our diet consisted of beans, potatoes, and tortillas, all things from the harvest of the land. In town, that was out the door. He had sold the land and opened up a bar as he said it was good business. However, he was drunk most of the time and his friends took advantage of this and eventually he went broke.

It was then that my parents having visas to visit the USA for work became a good thing, but this left me in charge of my siblings at just ten years old. My parents would come whenever possible to give us food, but as time went on, they left for longer periods of time. There was no longer food to feed us and I started knocking on doors asking for work doing errands. I was able to get some work and get some money for food for a while. Soon, as time passed, the neighborhood became just like us; things were hard for everybody. It was heartbreaking to hear my siblings cry because they were so hungry, and I couldn't feed them. Some days it was a good day, other days not so good. On occasion one of my neighbors, who was fifteen years old, taking care of her siblings, too, would call me and give me some cooked beans, where I would ration the food so that everybody could get some in their tummy. That went on for a while until one time while I was knocking on doors for work, I got sexually molested. I don't really remember much of what happened.

One day my parents came back and my mom, who was pregnant, delivered a baby boy. The baby was born sick and unfortunately had to stay in the hospital for some time. My parents decided to move us to the United States. In 1979, at the age of twelve, I ended up in Peñitas, Texas, as a friend of my father let us stay in a small cabin. I would cook for my siblings in an old oil drum barrel, and I had to search for wood in the area that was close by. My mom was working by cleaning houses and my dad was helping the owner of the cabin doing some handyman stuff. My mom then signed us up for school where I would graduate in 1987. I graduated from La Joya Independent School District, La Joya, Texas.

In 1989, I met the man who would become my husband, and in 1991 we moved to Oregon where one of my younger sisters was living. We started working in a potato processing plant to get settled down and we made friends quickly. We ended up working there for ten years. During that time, I noticed people would always make comments about the volume of my laugh, that they could hear me from the lunchroom on the second floor to the first. I remember the table where my friends and I would sit was always full to the point that people would try and make space to allow more people to sit with us. There was always laughter and just good times. When I finally got pregnant after trying for five years, the baby shower was held in the lunchroom, and it was packed with gifts. I am thankful for the love and support of my co-workers and friends.

I had my second daughter in 1998, and the pregnancy was so delicate that I was on bed rest for half of the pregnancy. By that time, I was feeling like I needed a change of scenery and I quit working. I somehow ended up applying for a position as a domestic violence advocate at a nonprofit organization when I felt ready to rejoin the workforce because they needed a bilingual person, so I applied. And by fate, I was hired and got sent to many trainings for two weeks and got a shared space with a clinic and it was just me in the office. My duties were to promote the services. I was busy doing public presentations and making alliances with other state agencies.

We opened another office in another town and just kept promoting the agency and providing the services in two locations. At first, it was hard seeing the clients with bludgeoned bruises, black eyes, and sometimes burns on their bodies. I could feel their pain. However, the spirit of my grandmother lived in me and I did my best to be a healer for them to the point that the District Attorney liked the job I was doing and asked me to facilitate the Men's Anger Support Group. By that time, I was already helping with The Women's Support Group. The DA decided to train me in collecting criminal evidence for some of the women's cases. I also was organizing a teen support group. I had a full work agenda, and it was just me with a portable computer and a printer. I loved the work. I got to help several women gather their paperwork to get their work permit through the Violence Against Women Act, which President Bill Clinton signed in 1994.

When I found out I was pregnant with my third child, and since I had had difficulty with my previous pregnancies as well as other issues, I decided to leave my job. I loved my work, but I was doing so much that I had to think of my baby's health and I moved back to Texas.

I worked at The Texas Migrant Council where I was a jack of all trades. Sometimes I would be a teacher's aide or a bus aide, since I'm good with talking to people. I gave school information to parents and loved doing the work.

I think growing up seeing my grandma healing people and my mom helping people, it became second nature for me to be helpful. If I can help someone, I will. There are different ways of doing it; a smile is a great way of making people feel welcomed.

I have experienced pain and suffering, but I have also experienced love and compassion. To me it's a decision to choose to focus on the good, the happy memories, the joy of life! I am responsible for my actions only.

I open my personal space to shift the energy wherever I am. It makes people feel safe and like they can express themselves. I only do it when whoever is there grants permission for it to happen. I have been doing this work for many years. I do personal assessments and I can pinpoint the needs through the speech pattern; everyone has a specific pattern.

I truly believe everyone has a healing gift to offer humanity. What's yours?

Maria Elena De Lira

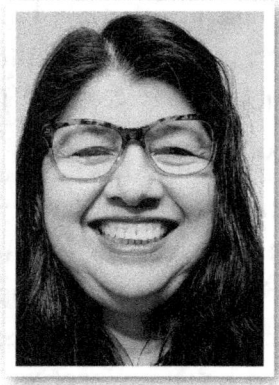

Maria Elena De Lira is a woman who loves to motivate and help people to see the best in themselves. She volunteered at the local school district, while her children were attending school; she volunteered at The Texas Migrant Council before she got hired by them; and she volunteered at Dress for Success.

Maria is trained in crisis intervention, sexual assault intervention, and also as a Domestic Violence Advocate. She has served as a member on several groups. She is also an International Bestselling Author.

Maria is a wonderful human being who always helps people, and she is on a mission to enrich people's lives with compassion and respect.

Connect with Maria at www.facebook.com/maria.delira.77.

CHAPTER 14

The Depth of a Woman's Healing Power

by Mary Elizabeth Jackson

I can't remember when I realized I had any healing power in this life. Power as a young girl, power as a young woman, then a woman, as a mother, wife, or any other hat I have ever worn, I've used it. Healing comes in many forms. What is true healing power? It is defined by each individual in the experience they have in this life.

I only understood this fully once I was an adult and after having my children. I was told once by a very wise woman that one of the most powerful things a woman can do is to raise a child. That can come in many different forms. The gift and privilege of loving another human being, guiding them, and helping them grow are some of the most precious, powerful, and sacred acts we can offer in this life.

Mothering for me changed as these words were spoken to me. I was told I could never have children. I was diagnosed with Polycystic ovary syndrome and thyroid issues in my early twenties, but didn't understand it or wasn't given much information about it over thirty years ago. I was married seven years before I got pregnant with our first child. I am still unsure how that happened because I had just started at the fertility clinic. The doctor hadn't used any techniques yet. I had been to hell and back with my hormonal and endocrine health, searching for years for help and healing. Four pregnancies and three children later, I believe in miracles, especially in the birth of my children. And the power of faith kept me going.

The healing power of love and faith has been present throughout my life, whether joyful, traumatic, or challenging. Understanding the depth and power of love and faith and their healing powers has led me down a different path. It has been with me through numerous trials, tribulations, and events I thought would be my end. I've had to have a never-ending and unbending faith and love in my life for times that included my children's entrances into this world. This power came from a place beyond me and required strength I did not realize I had within me.

From when I was a little girl, I knew and could feel a power that was present but unseen. It has always been there, pushing and sometimes carrying me forward. At times I have not understood what it was, but it has always been present like a steady stream or trusted friend. Now, I meditate, focus on this energy, and have taught my children how to tune into it. Knowing there is a power greater than ourselves helps us have a different respect for life and allows us to grow our awareness in all areas.

The healing power of love and faith has helped me through unthinkable events, from being raped by my boyfriend at sixteen to one of my children being abused in school when she was the young age of five. Both, as well as God, has played a significant role in helping me

148

get through and recover from events like this. There have been other challenges along my life path, and faith and love have come along on the journey.

As a little girl, I have always believed in God and wanted to be close to Him every day. When I was about ten-eleven years old, one night in my bedroom, I prayed very hard. My parents were divorcing, and I had just lost one or both of my grandparents, very close together. I was praying to feel God, know that He was real, and feel His comfort and love. Suddenly, this purple orb or circle of light was at the end of my bed. It was beautiful. I was not frightened. It started coming towards me, and then the light enveloped me. I began to cry. The feeling of this light all around me was like a big warm hug of love that I could feel throughout my whole body, saying, "It's going to be okay. You are okay, and you are loved, and I am real." I do not remember how long it lasted, but as it left, I kept asking the light to stay. I wanted God to stay with me always. I was crying and pleading. It was the first comfort I had felt in a long time.

I felt alone, and my room was quiet after the purple light left, yet I knew this love and power were real. God was real for me, and this experience would define many things. I spent a lot of time in the church till I was in high school. Then I overheard the adults gossiping. Some things occurred in our church that made me leave during my young adult years. It was a bubble that burst—man versus God. I knew my experience when I was younger was real, but what I saw from the world would challenge my belief in others and that I was safe.

My junior high and high school years were a divorced family-latchkey kid life. My mom worked full time to take care of my two brothers and me. I had to grow up early and help raise them, but my senior year of high school was very untraditional. My mother moved away because of a relationship she was in and took my brothers. I stayed behind to finish my senior year. I did not want to leave, so I lived with one of my best friends and her family. Her mother was one of my teachers in school, and we went to church together. I was born in Orlando and grew up in a smaller town in Florida where everyone knew everyone else, among the beautiful lakes. It was a safe place, and no one ever locked their doors at night. Our pastor lived on our street. We had one high school in the county, and where I lived there was a very small-town homey feel.

I spent a lot of time riding horses in the orange groves, and riding was a saving grace for me. I have always had this unique relationship with nature, animals, and children. It always seemed "normal" to me, and I never wondered about it. My mother would laugh and say broken things found their way to me. I was always helping or helping to fix someone or something. I would know something before it happened or hear it in my head. As I got much older, I learned I was an empath, highly intuitive, and psychic, some might say. We all have these abilities, but life and people sometimes teach us it's wrong or evil. I was raised to understand both the Christian world and what I call the "unseen" world. They co-exist in the same space at the same time. It is all a part of the same thing or energy God created or whatever you believe to be your higher power or understanding.

As the ability of intuition and empathy continued to get stronger, I began to feel like it was more of a curse than a gift. As an empath, you "feel" or can sense what other people are going through, sometimes physically and mentally. It can be very taxing and wearing on a person. When you meet someone, it's like a door opens, and you can see a movie of things about their life or know whether they are telling the truth or not. I call this my "God alarm"; we are all born with it, but we don't always know how to tune into it or utilize it. A "mother's intuition" is another name for it. This guide or intuition is helpful when

150

raising children or steering us away from a situation or person that may not be in our highest and best good.

My dreams became more vivid the older I got. I was a social butterfly, but sometimes being around others became impossible. I could hear the answer to a question before someone answered me. I found I needed more alone and "recharge" time. I did a lot of searching to understand what I had been experiencing since I was a little girl, and in time I grew to see this as a superpower. We all have the ability or capability of tuning into this, but some of us are born already tuned in.

I am sharing this because even through these experiences, I have had to turn to the power of love and faith to help guide me. These powers have helped keep me grounded when I needed to be. They helped me not give up when I wanted to or couldn't see the path clear ahead of me when I felt abandoned and unlovable and did not realize my self-worth. Faith, love, and God were always there. But we must decide in this life what our self-worth and value are, not what the world or others say it is. Whenever I have the opportunity to talk to kids or teach, I tell them, "Figure out whom you believe you are and what you believe to be true about yourself, not what someone else says or the world says." Your truth is the only truth. What's in your heart when you are quiet and still and can hear the whispers of love that rise from your own heart. That is the power that lies within each of us. Be brave enough to stand in our truth so that others around us can do the same thing. That's power.

When my father left, and I grew up feeling unlovable, not good enough, and abandoned, I sought approval from others. Many of us do in life. I ended up in a very abusive relationship in high school. My mother had moved away, and I was living with my best friend's family at that time. I could not see how abusive the relationship was nor knew how to get out of it. At that time in my life, I never wanted to displease anyone because I was afraid they would leave me and I would be alone.

It was an illusion, and I was too young to know the psychology behind my actions.

This relationship was abusive physically, emotionally, and mentally. My first sexual experience was forced, and I was threatened if I did not comply. No one knew any of this was happening. I had too much shame and fear. I look back on pictures of myself at that time and see that I hid behind a makeup mask. It sounds weird, but I guess in my young mind, this protected me. It was my way of hiding the truth because of the guilt I felt. My mother helped me as best she could, and in the end, that power within me rose inside me, and I was able to get away from that situation. He followed me until the day I married my husband and it took years for me to heal. Along the way, I learned so much about myself and why we, as humans, do what we do. This helped me understand others, free myself from being stuck in a place of trauma, and learn to trust again.

We all have dealt with challenges, difficulties, and loss, but it doesn't have to define us or keep us from moving forward. As a woman, we have so many gifts and blessings we are born with, and sometimes we can't see them. But we can heal and be more assertive with faith, power, and love. We can use what we have been through and help empower others that are going through the same thing we did or something similar. This is a power that lies within a woman.

I did not realize the strength I had till my middle daughter was abused in her classroom in pre-kindergarten for eight months. I received a phone call from the police department in March 2009 letting me know our daughter's teacher had been removed from the classroom and was under investigation. This was on a Sunday night, so I had to go through an entire night not knowing what had happened. Our daughter was not entirely verbal then, so she could not tell us anything. When I finally could get a hold of the investigator, I was told the teacher had been removed and was being investigated for physically, emotionally, verbally, and mentally abusing our daughter. My entire life changed when I listened to what he was saying. It did not seem real or possible. It was the beginning of years of lawyers, therapists, depositions, courtroom hearings, and a trial. It was the longest five years of my life and for our whole family.

At times it was too much for my husband to deal with; for me, a power rose again inside me and pulled me forward, never looking back. I went into survival mode. It was a place I knew too well. Keep going, find an answer, and solve the problem. Momma Bear went into full force. I had to do something; someone had to help and make this right. No child should ever be abused, not once ever! I began a journey to change the law in our state. Something good had to come out of something so horrible.

I marched up to Capitol Hill, where I live. I set up meetings with Senators, State Reps, disability organizations, and anyone who would listen or talk to me. I had no idea what I was doing at the time, but I was determined. It gave me a goal and something positive to focus on. My sweet baby girl had been broken at the hands of another person, and that would never be okay.

I am still praying for resolve to this day. What was an easy solution or at least might help was putting cameras in classrooms of kids with challenges and special needs. To me, it was a no-brainer and a win-win solution, not for the legislators and people in power. I wanted to help make something positive come out of this situation and at least try to save other children from finding themselves in the same situation. It proved more complex than I thought. At that point, I lost all faith in the justice system and mankind.

I share these experiences not because it is easy to talk about, but because I have gone through this and have come out the other side. The power of love and faith can heal more than we might ever imagine it will. That power has led me through my journey as a mother and helped my children recover from unimaginable trials, traumas, and struggles. Sometimes we have to be the power of love and faith that helps another person heal when they can't do it themselves.

Part of our job as a mother is to pour love and faith into our children so they can do it on their own someday. It helps to ground them so they know something bigger and more powerful is out there for them to lean on and draw strength from. Be the example of love and faith in their lives. Children emulate everything they see in their environment. It is our job to be brave enough to look at ourselves in the mirror and say, "Okay, what do I need to heal or fix about myself so I can be the best version of me I can be?" That is my gift. This is your gift.

Showing up in this life, even with cracks, wounds, and breaks, makes us more authentic and inspires others to do the same. Knowing we can heal and help someone else heal is empowering. None of us are perfect, but owning our truths is freeing. The power of faith and love can go beyond what we can see right in front of us and, on the other side, might be a deeper, richer life.

When I started my parenting journey, I never dreamed I would experience the things I have. All three of my children have had challenges; two were born non-verbal and on the spectrum. We are here on this side through God, love, and faith, and I am so grateful every day. My husband and I have never stopped or given up, despite any challenges or what our middle daughter went through. It was a very lonely and challenging time that no parent is ever prepared to deal with. I am happy to say that she is a freshman in college and doing well. She has triggers, and we deal with whatever comes up, but we have taught

154

her to believe in herself and that she is stronger and more powerful than what happened to her all those years ago.

It is an honor and privilege to be a woman and know the love, strength, and power that lives inside me. This is within each of us, and when we use it and share it with others, it helps them be strong, too. Saying yes to ourselves allows others to say yes to who they are. This allows that power to continue to grow. I am grateful for the powerful women who came before me in my family, showing me how to survive and thrive.

We must forgive ourselves and be willing to look deep within the cracks to see where our healing needs to begin. This is a way to honor ourselves and be the love, faith, and power we seek. Never give up, get quiet and listen to the voice that lies in your heart. It will tell you your truth and that you can get through whatever you may face, that you can heal and be the empowered woman you already are. Own that power, and be the light the world needs. This is my gift. This is your gift.

Mary Elizabeth Jackson

Mary Elizabeth Jackson is a four-time #1 Amazon Bestselling author in the collaborative anthologies *Glimpses into the World of Autism*, *The Fearless Entrepreneurs*, and International Bestsellers *Invisible No More; Invincible Forever More* (Aug 2021), and *The Book I Read* (March 2022). Jackson is also the 2017 Gold Maxy award-winning author of the children's book series *Perfectly Precious Poohlicious and Poohlicious Look at Me, Poohlicious Oh the Wonder of Me*, and *Cheers from Heaven*, a mid-grade reader with co-writer Thornton Cline.

Jackson focuses on writing empowering books for kids and adults. Jackson is also a ghostwriter, collaborator, educator, hit songwriter, the voice for the Sports2Gether app, co-writer for Open When and manager of singing duo Sisters J.

Mrs. Jackson is a special needs advocate and an Ambassador Advocate for AutismTn. Jackson is also an advocate advisor for the Global non-profit Billion-Strong. She co-founded and co-hosts Writers Corner Live TV, and Special Needs TV Shows that air on Amazon Live, Facebook, Twitter, LinkedIn, and YouTube. Writers Corner Live features author interviews from New York Times bestsellers, International and

National best sellers, multi-award-winning authors, and all things in the writing world. Special Needs TV features interviews and resources for parents, families, and caregivers. Jackson has a new author podcast called Cover to Cover. Jackson is currently working on an anti-bullying campaign as well.

Mrs. Jackson is a very busy mom, wife, empath, and intuitive. She loves nature, being creative, anything funny, and inspiring others to believe in themselves to go from where they are to their full potential. She lives with her hubby, three kids, and a dog in the Nashville area. Cherish every moment of life.

Connect with Mrs. Jackson at www.maryejackson.com.

CHAPTER 15

The Medicine of Winter

by Melissa Renee

We all come to a fork in the road, where the universe drops us off one day and whispers in our ear, "What are you going to do? How are you going to move forward?" With no judgment or interference, it watches as you observe your choices: one path leads you back to your authentic self, leading you to your soul's truth and knowing, and the other path, congested with all of the false illusions you had about life to include yourself. It was December 2020. I was in year nineteen as a U.S. Soldier processing the collapse of my marriage of nineteen years.

This was my dark season of the soul, where I was exposed to disturbing truths of my marriage, including all the suppression of my authentic self. It was also the time to rediscover my intimate relationship with Spirit and myself. It was the beginning of the end of unpacking all of this, and I realized quickly that there was a lot my ex-husband kept from me. Anger, bitterness, and spite flew about me like shards of glass during those first few weeks. I was feeling disrespected, gaslighted, and made a fool of.

159

Spirit's message got louder while I was standing at this significant junction in my life. I stood frozen for what felt like an eternity as the Universe asked me, "What now?" My ancestors were all sitting on the other side of the veil, anxiously waiting to see how I would proceed. I didn't even know if I would internally combust, be ridden with anger as the victim, or I would be the rising phoenix. I never thought I'd find myself here. We don't know until it happens to us. Even though Spirit tried hard over the years to send me signs, I didn't pay attention. Finally, the revealed truths were so shocking that I had to pause, acknowledge, and take action. And with that, the journey back to my soul's blueprint began – a healing journey to my authentic self.

I want to rewind a little before unpacking this moment so you can better understand who that woman was at the crossroads, for it was crucial in my healing journey and where I am today. In 2002, I left my waitressing job at the Hard Rock Cafe in Myrtle Beach, South Carolina, to join the Army. My time at Myrtle Beach ran its course, and it was time to think about my future. I had a bachelor's degree from Penn State in Accounting, yet I had no desire to be an Accountant. I wanted more; I didn't know what that was. My boyfriend (now ex-husband) and I decided to enlist in the Army together in 2002 for various reasons (pay off my loan from college, serve my country, and travel). We married in February of 2002, and I went to boot camp in March.

The military is a giant melting pot where you see all different types of people from entirely different backgrounds. Regardless of the motive, the purpose is the same – to serve. While living in Germany from 2002-2009, I deployed to Iraq for fifteen months and Afghanistan for twelve months. The military also sent me all over the U.S. after my time in Germany. I had some of the most deeply spiritual moments while deployed in a combat zone. During the quiet moments, I pondered my reasons for serving, life's grand design, the mystery of the universe, and the evolution of my soul. It is interesting to see how spirituality morphs when you are in a hostile environment thinking about your mortality when you hear rocket-propelled grenades and small arms fire. You feel alone, but also part of a collective, a family you serve with. Shoulder to shoulder, you stand with your brothers and sisters in arms, all going through the same thoughts: *Are my loved ones safe? Will I get home safe? Am I missed?*

After two decades of being in the Army, I can now reflect and see the kisses the universe was blowing at me. I was learning to be not only a Warrior, but also a Healer. While my vocation in the Army was as a Systems Administrator, I carry many more realizations and knowings due to all of my experiences.

I was initially exposed to Reiki after tirelessly trying to find a way to alleviate my ex-husband's pain while married. He had an L4-L5-S1 double spinal fusion in 2009 when his chiropractor said words like 'energy healing.' It excited me to learn more about what I could do to help my ex-husband and his pain. I started reading about different energy healing techniques like Quantum Touch and Energy Medicine. Learning what energy felt like was fascinating, but I was raw in learning as I was teaching myself. In 2012, I stumbled into a meetup Reiki group while living in Georgia, and that's when my Reiki teacher, a Shihan, found me. She suggested we both learn Reiki together to help each other. This was the most profound experience I have learned, and it was very empowering to learn this ancient style of facilitating healing. I realized in my training what a clairvoyant I was and what a strong conduit I could be for universal energy to flow through.

Over the years, I continued to practice Reiki (becoming a Master in 2015) and my ex-husband was the main person I practiced on. Expressing my love for Reiki was not an open and understandable concept at work, so I kept those conversations to myself. I noticed over the years that regardless of the location when people don't understand concepts rooted in spirituality, they tie words like voodoo or witchcraft to spirituality and energy healing. This would deflate my excitement, and I became more selective with whom I shared my gifts.

In 2019, I took a one-year training program that taught universal shamanic practices. After this training, I was gifted by Spirit a new gift: channeling through doodling. I learned that if I doodled before a healing session, I could pick up more information for the client. While I didn't know how this would come together in retirement, I knew three significant exposures in my life were shaping my future: being married to a man with Post Traumatic Stress Syndrome (PTSD) that also had debilitating chronic pain, being around a military community, and my desire to live a heart-centered, authentic life.

I found myself in love with the embodiment of duality – the ying and the yang, the feminine and the masculine, or the Soldier and Healer. Regardless of popular opinion, I was steadfast in the concept that both could exist; it is actually healthier that way. During the latter part of my career, my energetic field was feeling tugs on both sides of the masculine and feminine energies. Both sides were demanding my attention. I had someone mention to me last year, "Try to find out how the feminine shows up as a Soldier and how the masculine shows up as a Healer." This was very thought-provoking because it's a normal societal belief that you must be one or the other. I still sit with this statement to this day, even now retired. I might never have the answer to this, but thoughts like these open my perspective to concepts that would be perceived as fixed and unyielding.

As you can see, I had quite the spiritual and warrior journey when I got to the dissolution of my marriage in 2020. Those first steps would set the tone for my healing and what would come afterward. It was my choice whether I'd feel that medicine and allow all layers of me to digest it or take safe routes (like numbing myself or playing the victim). I didn't know how I would get through this divorce, but one thing was for sure – I would never repeat this. I knew I would have to do some serious soul work to ensure I attracted a relationship at a much higher level.

I metabolized my divorce by feeling it all, from screaming to crying. That was how I spent my 2020 Christmas holiday. I ended up tearing down the Christmas decorations and throwing the tree in the trash. It was a very lonely time in my life, but the energy of my home, including all those that lived in this home, and all the animals on the land, past, and present, were gently supporting me as I went through my plethora of emotions.

It was a season of quietness, darkness, and solitude. Winter forced me to sit still and be alone in my thoughts. Being at work, I just had to compartmentalize my emotions, and because I outranked most of my shop, I couldn't share all I was dealing with. So, I cried going to work, worked, and then drove home with chaotic emotions flooding my mind. Each day, though, the crying and anger dwindled.

My home was an old farm home, and it was just my four cats and me. It was sitting in the darkness that led me to the light. I was thinking of how I would move forward and began reflecting on my desire to be an energy healer after my military career. I knew I was just an imposter if I didn't apply what I had learned. I had a plethora of knowledge from training as a Reiki Master, Guided Energy Medicine Practitioner, and wellness studies. They say the greatest healers are the ones that healed themselves. This was my time to practice what I preached and work on myself.

It is common to hear people recommend journaling to get your emotions out of you, but I always struggled with that and knew that would not be of value. I started to think about what else and recalled the Stress Management class I had taken six months prior. There was a chapter in there called Art Therapy. I was so fascinated by Art Therapy that I spent one month interviewing people (six months before my divorce) who specialized in the field for the Veteran community. I was fascinated by the depth of expression in art and how much more it revealed than voice. I was learning how emotions are diluted with language. Ask someone to dance or paint their grief. You will see and feel so much more. With this knowledge, I thought I'd try this out, and every morning before work, I would do a daily art journal entry. I had no idea what I would sketch, and I'd let my hand guide me.

I did this every day and knew I was on the right track because I was very consistent, and my mind felt clear afterward. It was very meditative. After filling up my art book, I needed to go bigger and bought large multimedia panels from Hobby Lobby and tacked them up on my kitchen wall. Every night I would sketch and sketch. I would later call this my emotional purge out of anger, bitterness, spite, fear, and sadness. It was chaotic and messy, but also beautiful. I then bought a roll of drawing paper and placed about seven feet of it on another wall of my kitchen. I began drawing a six-foot artistic silhouette of myself – a woman with one arm reaching up to the universe, desperately trying to connect to God for help. Art became my translator in how I was feeling. It bridged the gap between art and language; learning my voice wasn't even close to the depth of my art. Words tend to dilute what one is feeling. I was quickly learning the power of creative expression.

Art was only one facet of my healing journey. I found that my sacral chakra needed deep healing. My friend once said, "There's a connection between the sacral and throat chakra. When you heal the sacral chakra, you are helping your throat chakra." This creative work helped me find my voice. I also began incorporating dance into my routine with spiritual music. Stockholm Artist Fia was very instrumental for me. Her music got me to dance through the joy and tears as I found myself dropping more into my body. It was prayer with movement! Here it was, praying with a full embodiment. Every aspect of my body was praying, releasing, metabolizing, and renewing.

Layers of healing were being added, and I had a dedicated morning and evening routine. Mornings were my art sketching time; evenings evolved into a small ceremony for myself. I would dance and sing to highly spiritual music, drop into stillness and meditate, and conclude with prayers and gratitude. I gave such deep gratitude to all the animals and critters on my land, the families that lived in this home, the elements, my ancestors, and those spirits that were chosen to walk this path with me on the other side of the veil. I call them my divine team.

It took around four months to get a solid routine down as a single woman with no man in the house. I had to learn to do things in the home that my ex-husband would typically do. The nights were still very quiet, but my daily routines kept me focused on my cause – to heal.

I was determined never to repeat a relationship like my marriage. I knew I had to work to bring a lover into my life that I knew I was worthy of. To come to this realization, I had to do shadow work. I had to unpack my part in the marriage and why I even attracted a man like him into my life. I realized quickly that I had lost my voice years ago, like someone had just put the mute button on me. What was I afraid to say? What did I want from a future lover?

I dove deep into books that discussed intimacy and all its facets, including its sacredness. It was the first time that I was being exposed to such depths of this subject and ignited what I desired for a future lover. Reading, dancing, praying, and meditating made me realize that I was very emotionally malnourished. All the beautiful textures of intimacy weren't flourishing while I was married. In late spring, I was done with these feelings, and new words started coming to my mind: satiating, yummy, salacious, and sultry.

Each week my mind was getting clearer. I was releasing all my grief, including forgiving my ex-husband and myself. I was consistent with my creative and spiritual rituals and was starting to regain my sovereignty, identity, and boundaries. My friend Cindy would tell friends interested in receiving Reiki from me that this was the best time to receive from me because I was shining bright. And, oh, was I ever!

One day in the late spring, I started typing. Thoughts flooded when I told my friend Cindy, "I think I am writing a book." With dedication, 26,000 words flew out of me, and *Facets of Love* was birthed, a healing memoir dedicated to how I healed myself. The writing allowed my journey to come together and realize how far I had come and how fast I did heal myself.

After my book was released on Amazon on June 1st, 2021, it was suggested by my friend Kerry, a Psychic Medium, to stretch my mind regarding creative writing. She saw me writing "fantasy," as she put it. My conservative mind just giggled about it at first, but after a few weeks, I thought, "What if I just try?" "How would I write a sex scene?" "How would I write with no inhibitions?" I had no clue. The moment I threw caution to the wind, Spirit showed me a vision of a woman in a cabin in the dead of winter. And with that vision, the words started to pour out of me, writing fiction telling a story of deep heartache, yearning, intimacy, and winter personified as a woman. It was profoundly healing, and while it is still a work in progress, it has gifted me enough tools to have deep heart-centered conversations with my future partner. Writing this fiction has given me the language back to expressing myself, and I am now more comfortable having deep, intimate conversations. It was therapeutic for me and a perfect addition to my art journey. Art was the translator for me to speak my truth until I had my voice. It also helped me find my way home to my most authentic self. Now, I have it back and look forward to many yummy conversations with my future partner.

I tell people to this day that my ex-husband was my greatest teacher. I would never have learned Reiki if it wasn't for him. I know I had to go through that storm to get to where I am now. I would never be this open in my heart if I didn't go through this, and I know this experience has propelled me as a facilitator of healing. When we work on ourselves, we elevate our consciousness, which directly affects our abilities as a Lightworker. It's funny to look back and see how my life unfolded for all my gifts to come online. Everything I went through was to make space to recalibrate all the energies in my body. Because of this, I can facilitate healings at a much deeper level. I processed grief, deployed in combat, found my voice through creativity, and discovered my desire for deep intimacy. I found beauty in embodying polarity and healing modalities that I can always use. I absolutely love facilitating healings, and while sometimes chaotic, the journey has been all divinely orchestrated. We all have the innate gifts to help heal the planet and everything living on it, it is just whether it is this lifetime to use those gifts. Reiki blessings in your life. From my heart to yours.

Melissa Renee

Melissa Renee is a retired Chief Warrant Officer from the U.S. Army, where she served for over 20 years. She is a Usui Reiki Master, Guided Energy Medicine Practitioner, board-certified Health and Wellness Coach (NBC-HWC), and an Author. She spent a total time of 27 months in a combat environment: Afghanistan and Iraq. During these high-stress environments, it drove her to learn more about holistic modalities to help with ailments for the mind, body, and soul. Being an Army Soldier and an Energy healer led her on a unique journey of recognizing the beauty of embodying polarity in her life.

Melissa Renee is also the author of the book, *Facets of Love*, a healing memoir of her divorce from being married for 19 years utilizing all the tools she acquired over the years. During this journey, Melissa found a powerful tool for her transformation healing – creative expression. She strongly advocates the creative process for expressing suppressed desires and suffering.

After serving in the U.S. Army as a Signal Warrant Officer, she returned to civilian life, moved to Destin, Florida, and began to focus on her passions: energy healing, wellness coaching, and writing.

Connect with Melissa at https://calendly.com/mrsyanni/90minutes.

CHAPTER 16

Spacious Presence

by Michel Spruance

A healer? Really?

I didn't want to be a healer. My ego really wanted to be an international human rights lawyer, or an elected representative, or any number of high-profile positions that would positively change our world.

Even today, writing this chapter, I don't claim to be a healer. I do claim, however, to have a gift of spacious presence to offer you.

In this spacious presence, I listen for your wholeness. In this presence, your whole story is welcome - your trials, your tribulations, your joys, your accomplishments, your strengths, your doubts, your fears, your wonderings - your whole being. It is also the kind of presence that listens through and beyond your story for your innate wholeness. In this presence, you tap back into who you are - fully, unapologetically, worthy, and complete.

I did not ask to have this gift, and I do not believe it is mine, nor that it comes from me. I certainly don't show up this way all the time, every day, in every interaction. I am, after all, a pretty normal human being.

Yet, I've discovered that what I most care about in the world - my mission so to speak - is to alleviate our individual and collective suffering. The tool I have been given is to hold you, dear friend, with your wholeness in mind, giving you space enough to be who you are here to be.

Pause. Feel that for a moment. What's possible in that space?

What does it mean to have a gift?

Look up the word gift in the Merriam-Webster dictionary you'll find two definitions:

1. "a thing given willingly to someone without payment; a present"

2. "a natural ability or talent"

Added together, these definitions feel like a gift not only for me to give, but also one I receive. My happy place is facilitating and coaching, curating spaces where you might feel what it is like to be whole, connect back into yourself, and experience yourself through and beyond your suffering. It is a space that gives you a taste of yourself sans the bitterness of the past, or the sour longing of the future, yet does not deny that suffering occurs.

This is the use of memory:
For liberation – not less of love but of expanding
Of love beyond desire, and so liberation
From the future as well as the past.
~T.S. Elliott, Little Gidding III, The Four Quartets

Unfettered by past and future, you and I, and we are free to be who you are here to be, even if for the briefest of breaths.

Sharing this gift is a flow state for me, much like skiing or playing in the mountains is. Nothing about this feels heavy or hard, and I don't try to make it happen. It is a gift that I give freely, and it is a talent that I've both unconsciously and consciously cultivated.

This is my dharma. While Dharma is a complex word with many meanings. It can be defined as sacred duty, order, or law, and it comes from the Sanskrit root to sustain. I use it to describe my sacred duty and my calling. When I drop into this spacious presence, it is sustaining both for me and for others.

Just as I have discovered this gift of spacious presence, each of us, you included, has a gift to give the world. Your gift is a perfect expression of both/and. It is at once your talent, your happy place, your joy, *and* it is a gift to all those who experience your talent. At this intersection lies this gift that is essentially you, and no one else. It magically points you toward who you came here to be.

The Phoenix Burns

Magic. Gift. Dharma. Purpose. These words all have a particular inviting ring to them. They tug at my heart and pull me toward them. On the one hand, being in this space of presence with others allows me to experience timeless flow. I love that part. It feels like joy and freedom and play. This is how I know this is my gift and I long to spend as much time there as possible.

On the other hand, living into my gift has not always been easy. In Stephen Cope's *The Great Work of Your Life: A Guide for the Journey of Your True Calling*, he shares a powerful insight that shook him years

171

ago: "If you bring forth what is within you, it will save you. If you do not bring forth what is within you, it will destroy you." (Note, this is Cope's riff off a quote from the Gnostic Gospel of Thomas.)

This sounds pretty severe. Yet, I've had my own brush with destruction at least twice in my life. I dare say these difficult times were necessary to help me embrace this gift.

The first time was in my early thirties. From a young age I knew that I was here on this earth to alleviate the suffering that stems from our sense of separateness. As a high school student in history class, my heart ached for the senseless tragedy of the human condition, much of which we bring upon ourselves. War. Famine. Abuse. Destruction of our planet, and the beautiful animals and diversity we get to live among. All this suffering broke my heart, as in a literal feeling of having my heart shattered. Even today, when I allow myself to feel deeply, that same sensation wells within me.

Off I went to college to become a history teacher with the intention of inspiring *all* young folks to become the citizens the world needs. I was especially passionate supporting teens who were less likely to be told their voices mattered.

I loved teaching, worked hard, and made a difference. I was honored to spend my days with young folks weaving their worlds together and asking important questions. Not one day was like the next. Most always, we enjoyed at least one full belly laugh. Classroom teaching was my first powerful calling and I was right to have listened.

Yet, after seven years, I found myself struggling each day just to get through the day. I felt depressed. The malaise was spilling into my life and my marriage. I was short tempered and not much fun. Most of the enjoyable things my husband and I did together turned into difficult conversations, leaving us feeling far, far apart, even as we sat right next to each other. I was scared.

I knew that classroom teaching was not my "it" anymore. Every day I thought, "how much longer can I do this?" I could not identify why it wasn't right anymore. On paper it seemed such a perfect fit for me. Yet my being was withering. No amount of intellectual discussion could change this. Something else was pushing in me to come forward and I did not know what.

It was destroying me, or at least my struggle with it was destroying me. Something new wanted to come through, yet without a clear pathway, I floundered. I struggled to know what to do next. I thrashed about, spending long hours reading jobs posts on the internet. (Note: if you find yourself doing this, something important may be knocking in your soul). Deeper and deeper I descended into a black hole, unclear how to get out and move forward.

All that I thought I knew, all that I believed to be true about my identity was coming into question, burring away, emptying me out.

The Wilderness

This is what I consider my first wilderness. That expanse of time and space where I wanted to know the answer, and the answer was not yet ready to be known. Like standing in quicksand, the more I struggled to find the answer, the deeper my sense of despair.

"Be patient toward all that is unsolved in your heart and try to live the questions themselves, like locked rooms and like books that are now written in a very foreign tongue. Do not now seek the answers, which cannot be given you because you would not be able to live them. And the point is, to live everything. Life the questions now. Perhaps you will then gradually, without noticing it, live along some distant day into the answer." ~Rainer Maria Rilke

The wilderness was indeed painful. So many questions and so much unknown. Should I go back to school and get a PhD? Should I change jobs entirely? Everyone had an opinion. Family shared their confusion and concerns. Why would I give up a profession where I had already gained respect and made a mark, especially in a field that seemed so noble?

This was a time of inner turmoil. It felt desolate. Barren. Interminable. A true wilderness with no clear pathway out.

This wilderness could take many forms, but must almost always be crossed as you grapple with your gift. It may appear as lack of clarity, self-doubt, other's opinions, depression, and countless other forms of struggle.

In retrospect, I understand that the depth of suffering I endured in this time was brought on by my impatience and sense that I should have the answer on my timetable, which is almost always yesterday. It was uncomfortable and yet, it was required.

Some part of me had to be destroyed in order for the new parts to emerge. My identity as a classroom teacher certainly had to die. I remember viscerally sitting on the floor of my old classroom, crying

174

buckets of tears as I cleaned out files. As I prepared the way for another teacher to take that space, I was preparing my heart for a new gift to come forward. That inner death and death of identity, I've learned, are always signs of a new chapter emerging. A new layer of the gift readying itself to shine through.

What I have learned is that when these metamorphoses begin, and I find myself in the wilderness again, the only thing to do is to become more and more still. To begin to ask the questions again. Each day I show up willing to be with the questions, my heart softens, anxiety releases, and I experience peace even in the unknown. What is my purpose? How can I serve? What is my right path? I begin, little by little, breath by breath, to live into the answers.

This too feels like a kind of magic, and magic, I've learned, cannot be hurried. It must allow the wilderness to become its own gift.

Fulfillment

Inevitably, the wilderness gives way to a clear path, keeping the journey moving forward. When I finally let go of my identity as a classroom teacher, it felt like a weight off of my back. I then turned my attention wholeheartedly toward teaching yoga, my budding love and passion of the previous few years. I had been teaching for fun while I was still teaching school, and I found again the joy and timelessness in this space that I know to be a hallmark of being in my dharma.

I started my own yoga company, developed corporate mindfulness programs, and eventually opened a large urban yoga studio in the heart of Amazon's Seattle headquarters. I ran yoga teacher training and coached individuals and groups. Each of these offerings was an avenue for giving spacious presence to all the participants.

For thirteen years, this yoga studio fed my soul and gave me an outlet for this gift of spacious presence and a testing ground for how to bring it forward in the world. In a very real way, this was the fulfillment of my transformation from classroom teacher to sharing my gift in the world.

I felt particularly proud of the fact that as the pandemic began in 2020, we were right there as a studio, ready to serve our students, teachers, and team in very real ways. We creatively provided regular classes and deeper learning experiences to bring people together, to celebrate community, to support one another, and to see each other through to the other side.

Remember to celebrate milestones as you prepare
for the road ahead.
~Nelson Mandela

That thirteen-year run, offering spacious presence to so many brilliant people in so many different ways was an incredible gift. I feel it now in my bones. I feel content and grateful. I feel peace and expansion in my chest.

Pausing to notice the goodness our gifts have given fills our cups, readying us for the road ahead, for the fulfillment of one dream is not the end. There is always an after the happily ever after.

And Again

The realization of one dream always gives way to something new, and the yoga studio and my intertwined identities were no different. One day in 2022, I woke up and said this is enough. I have done enough. It was time to sell the yoga studio.

"Some of us think holding on makes us strong, but sometimes it is letting go." ~Herman Hesse

Once again, I faced the questions. If I do not own this business, who am I? If I do not have this studio through which to share the gift, how do I do it? Yes, this identity of business owner and yoga teacher had to be burned to ashes. Yes, there was the familiar wilderness. I struggled to imagine what else my life could be and how else I could possibly share this gift. I again felt barren and lost.

It was then that I laughed. This was no different than the first time. It was time again to sit quietly in the wilderness, show up for the questions, and allow the next expression to emerge. While I have still struggled at times, I know to let the phoenix burn so that something new can arise from the ashes. This time, I have guideposts for how to cross the wilderness. As I walk this path again, I suffer, but less, and with more joy.

Of course, with each new wilderness, new discoveries unfold. This time, as I cross the wilderness, I see new vistas. In the past, I had always focused on sharing my gifts externally, with the outside world. Yet, in that cycle of owning the yoga studio, I became a mom. Now, having sat with my questions and returned again toward a new path, I see significantly that it is time to turn my gift upon my family and my close community. It is time to give freely to my family, what I now see, I had reserved for everyone else. No matter how else it unfolds in the world, this new pathway and the fulfillment of my dharma, will center my family at the heart of what I do.

Making Friends with Doubt

To the outside world, I often seem very confident and always ready with ideas. Yet, behind the scenes a tumbling waterfall of questions,

177

struggles, fears, worries, and strategizing swirls in my mind. Always, doubt dances nearby. She is a constant friend, although she often feels like a foe.

For me doubt pops up frequently and in different forms, and is never welcome. I don't like it. I know I should embrace it, and I just want it to stop already.

While I know in my bones that this gift of spacious presence is what I'm here to share, the how of it often gets tangled. How do I share this gift and live in the real world? What does it look like to make a difference while making a living? How do I raise kids and bring to bear what I can imagine in the world?

Sometimes the doubt makes me think I am crazy. Like, this gift that I want to share is a bit weird, and what if my friends really knew what I thought about this gift? I've kept it hidden at times, and only really shared in the places I think I'll be one hundred percent accepted.

"Your task is not to seek for love, but merely to seek and find all of the barriers within yourself that you have built against it, and embrace them." ~Rumi

---

Yet doubt, like the questions Rilke speaks of, can become the very tool I need to move forward. Embracing doubt, I've learned to pause and notice her. When I feel the grip in my belly, the tightening in my throat, or the knot of anxiety in my chest, I pause. I acknowledge, "oh, there you are today." Then I ask, "is there something important you are trying to show me or tell me?"

Again, like magic, things usually shift. Most often, when I take the time to acknowledge the doubt and embrace it, it fades away.

Sometimes, the pause allows me to see something I wasn't seeing. Sometimes, in the pause, I just laugh.

Learning to dance with doubt has transformed her from a barrier to a gift, to a friend along the pathway and expressing my gift is the highest form of love I know both for the world and for myself.

Let Your Light So Shine

"Let your light so shine before men." ~Matthew 5:16

It is easy to hide our gifts. Yet, dear reader, your gift is the most important thing you can share in this world. It will be your expression of the greatest love, of your greatest dharma.

Even as I write this, I feel the tenderness that I, too, need to hear from time to time.

The world needs us. Let us each share our unique and sacred gifts with the world.

Michel E Spruance

Michel E Spruance (M.Ed, E-YRT 500) is an executive and small business strategic coach, helping leaders reach their goals and create new levels of success and excellence. Michel draws on a unique blend of traditional strategy, coaching, systems thinking, and the science of peak so that individuals, teams, and businesses reach new heights.

Committed to helping people build their business while they make a positive impact in the world, Michel brings twenty plus years as a teacher, facilitator, and coach, supporting individuals and teams. She is both compassionate and to the point. She ensures you move forward, while having fun and living fully.

Michel brings her background in a range of modalities, from business and somatic coaching to mindfulness and yoga. She is a certified coach with Lightyear Leadership, as well as Shift Positive 360. She has made harnessing your neurobiology and mindfulness a foundational tool for leading business, drawing on her training in the two-year MMCTP program, the Chopra Center, and more.

Michel has owned and run small businesses since 2006. Most recently she sold her successful yoga studio in downtown Seattle after thirteen years. She is also a co-founder of Space Between, a non-profit that facilitates educational transformation through school-based mindfulness in Washington State and the author of *Emerge Mindfully: Less Stress and More Joy from Difficult Times*.

Michel lives with her husband, kiddos and four-legged friends on Bainbridge Island, Washington, where she loves listening to the birds, playing in Puget Sound, and exploring the mountains and forests.

Connect with Michel at www.badasshappyhuman.com.

CHAPTER 17

The Energy Architect™

by Nasirra R Ahamed

Some changes look negative on the surface, but you will soon realize that space is being created in your life for something new to emerge. ~Eckhart Tolle

---

I can only marvel at how far I have traveled- Mentally, Emotionally & Spiritually.

You don't have to carry the past on the new path you're on. This new path is *today*. To understand where I am today, I must appreciate everything that made me who I am today. For that, I'm going back to the inner source and the time operating from *Where did this all begin?*

Have you ever wondered why you are here?

I'm Indian. My father worked in Bahrain and that is where I grew up with my parents and little brother. I lived in my small mind with my

183

limited exposure. We were not conservative and were fairly well to do. My Parents didn't try to hold me back or take the path for me, but they did do their job to light the path with their love and discipline, so that I could always find my own way.

Finding my own path took time. While growing up, I felt different and not enough. As the older child in the family, I did enjoy some privileges. However, I often felt a little overlooked and alone. I constantly needed security and emotional support, but did not know how to ask for it. This lacking didn't only influence who I was on the inside, but also played out in my relationships with people as I grew. The patterns set for me as a child dictated how I related with people growing up.

I developed severe acne in my teens which did not clear up till my mid-thirties, leaving scars and deep pits on my face. Acne is a condition that is more than skin deep. It can lead to magnified feelings of depression and social isolation. That's when my struggle for self-acceptance started. I personified this condition and gave it permission to deactivate my conscious decisions and defenses. My image in the mirror was hard to bear and I had had enough of taking pills and putting on miracle creams. I was constantly aggravated by the teasing, taunting and my face being scrutinized everywhere I went. That was the beginning of my relationship with shame and feelings of low self-worth. I allowed my skin's imperfections to define me. Every emotion that I suppressed, resurfaced only to further blow up. It negatively impacted my school life and my relationship with friends and family. I tried desperately to cover this up so that I could feel more accepted, which eventually turned me into a people pleaser. It was a protective coping mechanism to stay safe around others and to be attached to them. When we grow up in an environment where we consistently, directly or indirectly get the message that something is wrong with us, we abandon ourselves and focus on others instead. Just to stay connected to others, I abandoned myself to suppress my feelings, needs, wants, and desires. I projected my self-worth with other peoples' projections and their capacities. My skin still carries memories of where I've been.

When I was sixteen, I relocated to India with my brother. We were living on our own without my parents. I was on my own for the first time and thought that I had the opportunity to experience life on my own and see it through my eyes. I thought I was free and that I was starting a new life.

You will, however, continue to see the same emotional experience, creating a pattern. Until you change course and awaken to free yourself from your conditioning. I cannot thank my brother Nizam enough for his support during this time. It's been a great journey growing up with him and he was brave and stood by me even though he was just a child himself. I wished I could have been a better sister. Nothing gives me more pleasure than watching him grow up to be the accomplished handsome man he is today.

While all this was happening, I managed to scrape through college. I landed my first job in media and advertising. It's not what I'd planned, but I happened to be at the right place at the right time. A friend told me about a vacancy and I simply showed up for the interview and the rest is history. I did not tell my parents that my first job involved sales; it was drilled into us as children that only doctors, engineers, scientists and lawyers were respectable professions. I was good at my work, but was ashamed at the same time. If anyone asked me about my work, I would be vague about the nature of my job. It took me twenty-one years to break this childhood conditioning and figure out that I am more important than what job I do. A healthy sense of self is rooted in character, not career choice.

I was sincere and I worked hard. Respect and recognition made me feel good and motivated. I overheard my bosses say that I was good and even intelligent! Wow, intelligent? I had not experienced respect and recognition, I loved the feeling. I was finally good at something! I kept working hard, which led to promotions. I started to find some emotional stability. I finally felt in control of my life. I was offered better jobs with better roles. This motivated me to complete my Masters in Business Administration and I moved to senior roles. Success in my career was coming to me abundantly and I was getting financially and emotionally stronger. At thirty-four, I was the Assistant Vice President of a large media company. I started feeling confident. Everything that I felt was lacking in me, I made up through my work. Success and power became extremely important to me. It became my only identity.

I believed that this was what I was meant to do, to be a successful, powerful corporate leader.

Everything was going great. My life merged with a wonderful man during this time and nine years later, Radhakrishna & I married. It is true that when you are vibrating high, you do attract people and things that vibrate at your frequency.

Social theory maintains that children learn through imitation. Aggression is sometimes a conditioned response to neutral stimuli like social embarrassment, unfamiliar people, etc. It was difficult replacing old patterns of defending, withdrawing or attacking in the face of judgment and criticism. My process of language and communication was aggressive. It was a learned and automatic response. While I did not consider the way I spoke to be violent, my words would often cause hurt and pain to others, as well as myself. I simply did not know compassionate communication! I often wondered why what I said was always misinterpreted, and people reacted negatively. I was unable to articulate any observation without introducing judgment or evaluation.

Every conversation resulted in an escalated disagreement with emotions running high. Like a pendulum, I was oscillating between being a desperate people pleaser and being excessively aggressive.

My attachment to being the alpha female was great for business in corporate, but this was the most detrimental thing when it came to me attracting healthy relationships. There is a Yin and Yang to everything, there is a masculine or feminine, there's a light and a dark. When we are operating as an alpha female, one is operating in their masculine energy, because our feminine energy is probably wounded. It never learned that it was safe to flow. It doesn't know how to trust. So we step into this need to control, which ends up only on the other side of that Yin or Yang. It was time to stop treating my relationships like business.

This did not help any of my relationships. I was unable to let go of that which was modeled on me as a child. My career was going great and I felt that I was in control; however my teams felt I was a rigid task master. My personal relationships started getting strained. My relationships with my parents, in-laws and even my husband were stressed, which resulted in many clashes.

One year into my marriage, I delivered my son, Roshan. Roshan means light and fame in Hindi. I wanted to be there for Roshan and watch him grow. I went on maternity leave and for the first time, I was not working. Postpartum depression is a real thing. The depression caused more strained relationships in the family. I felt overwhelmed. I didn't have anyone who understood what I was going through. Things were falling apart. I did not have a support system to look after my son and I let go of my job as it involved travelling. I had built a strong structure of my career to protect me, thinking that that is what would make me strong. I believed that success in my career and finances would nullify everything in my past. I did not have the crutch of my career now, either. Now, when I reflect, this structure could have never stood for long, because there was no strong foundation to hold it up. Everything looked great from the outside, but the inside of me was empty. It was time to do the inner work and BUILD the foundation.

The more tension you felt as a child, the more life stress, overthinking and weight gain issues you will experience as an adult. You learn to constantly brace for danger and live with your guard up. As an adult you get overwhelmed by things quickly and you are offended easily, because living in survival mode instead of being relaxed in your body has become your norm. If your parents had high expectations of you, you now feel crushing amounts of career stress because deep down you are still trying to prove yourself. If your environment was very critical, angry or abusive, you are likely to become a very anxious people pleaser or an angry narcissist. The reason you overthink and are indecisive is because you felt that you were never quite good enough for them.

If you don't heal the root of any problem, it won't get resolved. Instead, it will either get worse or appear as another symptom. ~Teal Swan

---

Roshan was born to show me the light.

It was in those darkest moments that I connected with the source. I was broken and I needed healing. All I knew was that I was going to do everything in my power to become un-broken.

Healing is not becoming the best version of yourself. Healing is letting the worst version of yourself be loved.

Who you are is not your fault, but it is your responsibility.

In 2011, my journey into energy work started as one of learning to control. I thought I could HACK my energy and others' energies and beat them into submission. I wanted to learn how to override my stress responses. This, thankfully, changed during the course of my spiritual journey. The first few months were great and I learned to connect the dots, uncovering my patterns and conditioning. However, this is healing at a very superficial level.

The trauma I had stored in my body and nervous system wasn't allowing me to step into a life of abundance, because I was constantly operating from a place of fear. I was in a constant state of an amygdala hijack where my brain signaled danger and pumped stress hormones, preparing my body to either fight for survival or flee to safety at even the slightest trigger.

I was self-sabotaging myself; hiding and suppressing my own feelings and needs. I would stay in unhealthy relationships knowing that they are bad for me, hoping that someone will come and rescue me. I'd easily fall prey to my imposter syndrome. I would fall for peoples' potentials- not who they really are and how they really act or treat me and I would take on more than I could handle. I would blame others for my situation. I would either be the perfect people-pleaser, seeking validation and approval afraid of conflict or go to the other extreme of taking every conflict personally and getting agitated. I wanted my state of mind and relationships to be in balance and harmony. I was vibrating at a low frequency and thus attracted similar energies and experiences into my life. Positive vibrations are high frequency energy or emotions that are associated with happiness, peace, love, and overall well-being.

You learn that you are all of the resource and it all starts with you.

Energy healing is a holistic practice that involves the manipulation and balancing of the body's energy fields in order to promote healing and overall well-being. It is based on the belief that the body has its own natural healing ability and that certain techniques can be used to enhance this ability and remove blockages in the energy pathways. Examples of energy healing practices include Pranic healing, Reiki, acupuncture, etc. I started with Pranic Healing and eventually started learning other forms of Energy work.

Pranic healing is a form of energy healing that was developed by Grandmaster Choa Kok Sui. It is based on the concept of *prana*, which is a Sanskrit word for life energy or vital energy. The practice involves the use of specific techniques such as visualization and meditation to balance the body's energy fields. Disease and illness are caused by imbalances or blockages in the body's energy field and these imbalances can be corrected by removing the blockages and balancing the energy. These diseases and illnesses could be physical or emotional.

Chakras are centers of spiritual energy located along the spine. There are seven main chakras, each associated with specific physical, emotional and spiritual states. They regulate the flow of energy in the body and impact physical and mental well-being. Balancing the chakras leads to physical, emotional and spiritual harmony.

When chakras get blocked, they lead to physical, emotional and spiritual imbalances. These blocks can be caused by factors such as trauma, emotions or thoughts. Clearing these blocks restores balance to the chakras and improves overall health and well-being. Techniques used to clear chakra blocks may include meditation, yoga, energy healing, or affirmations.

Some beautiful paths cannot be discovered without getting lost. ~Erol Ozan

---

Spiritual awakening… We come under the veil of forgetfulness as we come into these physical bodies. At birth, we are compressed light into a density that consists of our actual soul aspects. But as we go through life, this is further reinforced by limiting beliefs in programming that we pick up in school, in religion and in our relationships. One day in the future you might start to feel this emptiness within you. There is a knowing, this longing for something greater that cannot be found when looking out into your external reality. That is a moment of a spiritual awakening. You will start to slowly reconnect with your divine self. Your soul aspect, your Spirit, and that will start to come through that veil of forgetfulness, that brick wall that kept you separated from this aspect of you, this greater aspect of you will start to dissolve. Finding your true self is active love.

Each person in your life is a teacher. Each experience in your life is a lesson. Attracting what's right for you will require you to finally let go of what isn't. I broke completely before I started building myself again with a strong authentic foundation.

My meditations, learning and practices started getting deeper. I started letting go of everything that was holding me back. I let go of friends that didn't share the same values and every belief that wasn't in alignment with who I wanted to be. I opened myself to the abundance that was meant for me.

I chose friends who wanted more for me, not from me.

Two years ago, I started recognizing that, after spending twenty-one years in corporate work, this career wasn't fulfilling me any longer. I had started gravitating to the world of personal development with the goal of retraining the brain to develop new neural pathways that support positive thinking, healthy habits, and overall well-being. I was intrigued by the different ways of changing negative thought patterns and behaviors through conscious effort. Mindset work and coaching alone are sometimes not sufficient to help people overcome their traumas and limiting beliefs. Many emotions and traumas are stored in the mind and body, especially the nervous system, which needs healing and somatic therapy. Trauma lives in the body and not always in the cognitive brain.

I integrated methods such as Cognitive Behavioral Therapy-CBT, Mindful practices, Neuro-linguistic programming- NLP, stress management, somatic therapy, Emotionally Focused Therapy - EFT with my Energy work to design & architect one true potential.

I began to realize that I had a deeper calling that was more aligned with who I was becoming. That voice got stronger. I was not sure how or when.

I decided it's time to own it here and speak about my story, because I know that this chapter in my life was meant to provide me with lessons and insight that I drew from, as I guide my clients in the future.

I invested the last two years in intense studies, certifications and research to be able to speak my dream into reality. I had no idea how I was going to do it. All I knew was that I wanted to help people through the life-changing work I had begun doing for myself.

I had found my purpose.

I am becoming. What I am becoming is authentic and intentional.

I integrate Coaching & Psychology with Ancient Energy Healing to Architect one's personal energy to realize and reach their true potential.

My brainchild, **Energy Architect™** is something that I'm now ready to present to the world and to the universe.

I am a Certified Coach

A Mind Reset & Rewiring Engineer

A Spiritual Scientist

A Specialist in meditation and Chakra Healing.

I am a Healer.

I am the Energy Architect™.

I am Nasirra R Ahamed.

Atma Namaste

Nasirra R Ahamed

Nasirra R Ahamed is an International Coaching Federation Certified Coach and the founder of "Energy Architect™".

She is an Executive Coach with over 21 years experience in Leadership roles. She completed her Masters from the prestigious Indian Institute of Management. Driven by empathy and defined by excellence, her Mission is to help Future Leaders, Organizations and Individuals Unleash their Potential.

Her Purpose is to Inspire, Lead & Transform.

She is a Certified Coach, a Mind Reset & Rewiring Engineer; a Spiritual Scientist; Healer. She specializes in meditation and Chakra healing.

Through her courses, coaching and writing, Nasirra integrates Coaching, mindset reprogramming, spirituality, somatic therapy, energy work and her intuitive gifts to help her clients clear limiting beliefs to unleash hidden potential to drive breakthrough results for themselves.

Her particular area of expertise is helping women, men, young adults and students, who feel lost, stuck or unclear about their next step, reconnect to their authentic self and purpose to create lasting freedom and fulfillment.

Her unique coaching philosophy and blueprint achieves results by igniting and strengthening a leader's inner and outer-cores, which enables them to realize "game-changing" outcomes that they can leverage in their business and life.

She offers one-on-one, group coaching and workshops to Architect a mindset for infinite energy and Intelligent Leadership to achieve sustained greatness.

She is the "Energy Architect™"

Connect with Nasirra at https://nasirra.com.

CHAPTER 18

How to Take the Journey to Heal

by Rita Farruggia

Healing our past emotional wounds is essential in order to be fully present in the moment and show up fully for life. If you don't recognize and process your traumas, they will continue to show up in your life in different forms and/or in different people. Not until you identify the roots of that painful experience are you going to break negative patterns. This chapter will discuss how I got stuck in a pattern of narcissistic abuse and how I got unstuck to break that pattern of familiarity.

I never recognized it until I had had enough of giving too much of my energy to narcissistic relationships, friendships, and romantic relationships. It wasn't until I left a long-term relationship with a narcissist that I recognized that I would stay in these types of relationships because it felt familiar. It felt familiar because I grew up in narcissistic family dynamics that led me to becoming a co-dependent. This is how my life became conditioned. I was conditioned to neglect my own needs and not recognize them. Instead, I solely focused on pleasing others. Also, those

197

who were uncomfortable with my strength of focus and determination to achieve my goals bullied me. So I know how others feel when narcissists try to put them down or covertly attack them.

I never focused on my abusers. I remained focused on my path through studying hard at school and participating in after school activities like volunteering, working at summer jobs and internships. I always kept busy. I never talked about it or gave it too much attention. I moved out of the family home without ever giving it much thought, only to continue to recreate those family energetic patterns over and over again. People took my energy and never gave much, if any, positive energy back. I was the one always there for the narcissist and the narcissist would not be there for me.

This was a pattern I experienced over and over again. I was the one to always help and show up in any way I could, and it was not a mutual, genuine relationship. The narcissist only loved what I could provide them, not me as a person. I grew up with the covert conditioning that my worth was tied up in helping those around me. This is what I had normalized and I carried it into my adult life without even recognizing it, that was until I was in a trauma bonded relationship with a malignant narcissist.

In order to cultivate the strength to leave the romantic relationship with the narcissist, I had to learn why I stayed. I stayed because I was familiar with this relationship dynamic. Then, in order to break this cycle, I had to learn how to love myself fully like my life depended on it. I had to uncover the inner psyche mechanisms that I developed while growing up, the need to focus solely on achieving and taking care of others' needs without even acknowledging my own. I never gave my needs any attention because I didn't even know what they were.

We end up recreating similar relationship dynamics as adults if we haven't healed the ones from our childhood. To stop trying to change the original source of the pattern, we unconsciously try to change other narcissists around us. The first step is recognizing that and really understanding it. We have to be honest with ourselves in order to self-reflect to process the original trauma, so we stop recreating it and release it from our nervous system.

To achieve self-reflection, you have to go back in time while your nervous system is in a relaxed state. You can then tap into your subconscious mind to allow you to go back in time to re-experience those traumatic events. Ask yourself important questions like, "Who did I have to become because of that event?" "What did I choose to believe?" "What did I learn from that event?" I like to do this self-reflective work while taking a long, hot bath. The warm water along with natural bath salts, natural bath bombs, natural essential oils like lavender enhance muscle relaxation so it is much easier to be in a meditative state to do inner work. This helps you process and release what is no longer serving you and stop familiar damaging patterns of behavior. You want to ensure you use natural products on your body because products that contain toxins will penetrate into your bloodstream, thereby putting toxins into your body. Toxic buildup in your body can lead to fatigue, headaches, insomnia, digestive problems, cloudy thinking, feeling sluggish, and the list goes on. On the journey to healing, we want to ensure we purge all toxins from our life (toxic products, toxic people, toxic thoughts, toxic programming, toxic energy, and toxic beliefs).

Secondly, I had to show myself love instead of relying on external people to feel loved. Part of being able to break free from a narcissist is being able to love yourself and to have the belief that you are worth having a healthy and genuine, real, loving relationship. Narcissists form a trauma bond with you, meaning you do experience cycles of love bombing from them from time to time, moments of love gestures with acts of deep care at times, only to meet with negative cycles of punishment or tearing you down. You stay during the bad cycles because you know the good cycle is coming afterwards. The conditioning means the good cycles keep you hooked into their abuse.

To break my own cycle of being trapped by the trauma bond, I committed myself to self-care to show myself self-love. This sent a subconscious message to my brain that I am worthy because I am responsible to feel good and joyful through my own actions. I have committed myself to a daily skincare routine using all natural facial masks. I combine it with saying daily affirmations in the mirror, "everyday in every way I am getting better" as I apply my all-natural skincare. As I wait for my facial mask to dry, I take the time to meditate. I lay down with crystals in the palms of my hand, on my chest, forehead, stomach, and around me while my aromatherapy diffuser is diffusing natural lavender oil. I meditate in silence for fifteen minutes until I wash off my facial mask. Viola, I have accomplished three things in one time slot: skincare, affirmations, and meditation. That is how I start my day every day. This is so powerful and gives me inner peace, clarity, inner joy, and the determination to focus on the good things in life and the good things I can create in life. This is so much better than focusing on negative things I cannot change. The powerful results from this newly adopted routine is one of the primary reasons I created Happybeingwell. com. I love helping people who want to create Zen in their mind, body, spirit, and home environment. Plus, I love the convenience of having amazing natural products for self-care all in one place.

Practicing self-love is important for laying a solid foundation in our lives so we can say no to things or people that are bad for us and say yes to people and things that are good for us. Also, what I just described above is a self-discovery process to reveal our true selves and allow our true selves to shine bright in our day-to-day life. We need to go on the journey of self-discovery to reveal how our traumas, whether small or large, have impacted on who we choose to become so we can deal with the internal factors to show up as a better version of ourselves. When we do this, we make better choices in life. We have more energy and a better mental vision to see more opportunities to go after in life. We live in faith instead of fear-based thinking that keeps us playing small. It's important that we go on this self-discovery journey because then we can also identify limiting beliefs that keep us stuck in life.

Third, we have to have compassion for ourselves for not fully seeing how our past molded the choices we made in life. You must learn to forgive yourself. Make this a part of your mantra on a daily basis. "I forgive myself for not knowing better. Now I know better so I will do better." Say it over and over again as part of your meditation mantra. I love saying mantras. I immediately feel better because I feel an immediate release of any negative energy in my body to feel lighter and happier when saying mantras. Say a mantra out loud now. Say "I feel good about myself" or "I send back any bad energy; I only accept and receive good energy." Notice how your body feels afterwards. You feel lighter and more grounded.

Becoming more aware of our bodily sensations helps us increase our self-awareness. Recognize and listen to what we are really feeling and experiencing in our body instead of focusing on the external world around us. Humans have between 60,000 to 90,000 thoughts a day and most people have negative thoughts. Therefore, this is an important practice to exercise daily; it helps you to listen to your intuition as well. So, when you catch your body not feeling right about something, listen to it, don't let the mind start debating with your gut instinct. Most people don't listen to their gut instinct because they are afraid that they are wrong. That is when you slowly tune it out.

Here are a few simple ways to tune into your body when you are watching a movie or a TV show. Pay attention to what your body is doing. Are you breathing from your chest or your belly? Are your muscles tense? Is your heart beating fast or slow? Is your body feeling relaxed? Also, practice tuning into your body when you are waiting in line at the grocery store or walking around the park. Just start observing your body on a regular basis.

Try yoga. It is therapeutic because you are tuning into your body in order to concentrate on holding each pose. Plus, you are feeling the strain of holding some challenging poses and you feel the contrast of deep relaxation with relaxing poses such as child's pose. Plus, some yoga poses help digestion and there are other health benefits associated with some yoga poses. Practicing yoga regularly (like meditation) increases your mental concentration, focus, and energy. I always feel great after a yoga session. It is a healthy way to release stress and experience joy because it is a form of exercise. You don't have to be an advanced yogi to practice yoga regularly. You can simply practice basic poses like warrior pose, downward dog, chair pose, and child's pose for ten minutes a day. If you want to add more as time goes on, that is up to you. You can do them in the comfort of your own home on a yoga mat. On my Happybeingwell. com blog, there are blog articles demonstrating basic yoga poses with picture demonstrations. You can do all of these poses at home.

More and more, people are recognizing the benefits of releasing trauma from their bodies. You may have heard that most people put stress in their back, hence why back pain is common in most people. Yoga is an excellent way to release trauma from the body. One practice I like to do when I meditate is I picture any negative energy in the form of black rays leaving my body and going up into the ethers to vanish from me. I hold a selenite crystal wand in my hand to hover over my body to cleanse my energy. Selenite crystal is a powerful energy cleanser. In fact, if you place other crystals on selenite, it cleanses your crystals. Selenite doesn't need cleansing.

Also, getting into the practice of identifying what your needs are in a situation or a relationship is an effective way to recognize your needs more easily. First, start writing them down on paper to yourself. Journaling is a powerful exercise to start getting your thoughts out of your head and onto paper. It helps to process thoughts, experiences, and emotions. Then become comfortable communicating your needs to others. At home, if you feel you are taking on too many tasks and feeling overwhelmed, share this with your partner and say for example, "I feel overwhelmed and would love and appreciate if you would take out the garbage. This will allow me to focus more on helping our children with their homework." Joining a support group where you can talk about your thoughts, feelings, experiences, and needs with others is very empowering to encourage you to do your inner work daily. In fact, Happybeingwell.com offers a free self-care support group, you can sign up on the self-care support group web page under the blog section.

What I've discovered is that once I cultivated a healthy relationship with myself using the practices mentioned above, my nervous system moved into a state of peace and calmness, instead of being addicted to the feeling of drama, chaos, confusion, and living in fear-based thinking. I became more empowered, calm, faith-based thinking, and attracted to people that are mentally and emotionally healthy and capable of true love. I learned how to live in my truth because I now know the truth of who I am through my self-discovery journey. This has made me unstoppable to living in my truth and no one will be able to convince me otherwise. I now live in conviction because I am living in my truth. My values and beliefs are congruent and I have the fuel to drive me into making my desires happen.

When you work on healing so you can heal, then you can live happy being well.

Rita Farruggia

Rita Farruggia is a self-care/self-love/happiness expert. Rita is the founder & CEO of happybeingwell.com, which is a wellness e-commerce site devoted to providing organic self-care products to amplify your wellness so you can be happy being well. HappyBeingWell.com has a mission of being the #1 Self-Care Community in North America.

Rita's mission is to awaken people to their love, teaching them how to reprogram their subconscious to align with truth through creating a daily self-care practice. It is through a commitment to a daily self-care practice that we can eliminate the noise of the world, stress, anxiety, and our rapid thoughts. This allows us to be able to align with our personal truth, love, clarity, focus, intuition, and confidence. This process allows us to know who we are and deepens our compassion and ability to love ourselves and others. This is the reason Rita is committed to providing the best natural products you will love to use and wear whether it's luxurious active-wear leggings to work out or meditate in, clean skincare, or creating a luxurious at-home spa feeling with salt lamps, crystal bookends, aromatherapy diffusers, natural essential oils, natural candles, all natural facial masks, crystals, and much more.

HappyBeingWell.com offers the tools/products, free educational resources, and inspiration to use in your daily spiritual and wellness practices.

Check out Rita's products at www.HappyBeingWell.com and use code "Healer10" to get 10% off any all-natural facial mask, all-natural essential oil, aromatherapy diffuser, all-natural bath salts, all-natural bath bombs, or crystal(s).

While on her website, pick up a free copy of her self-care journal, check out her blog, and get a free copy of her Meditation Made Easy ebook. Check out the Happy Being Well Podcast on Apple iTunes or Spotify.

—◆—

CHAPTER 19

Boldly Pursuing My Gifts

by Sally Green

Ever since I can remember, I have had a connection to spirit. I was a deep thinker and very curious, even at five years old. So much so, that one day I decided to reach out and speak to God directly! With determination, I picked up the telephone like it was no big deal and dialed the operator. This was a time when rotary dials reigned supreme and there was actually a live person on the other end. My mission was simple, to speak to God himself! That mission was thwarted by my mother who walked in as I was demanding that the operator connect me to God. Looking back, I realize that even though my attempt at using technology as the bridge to the divine failed, that experience served as one of my first steps towards spiritual growth. That curiosity and the desire for spiritual connection has been with me my entire life.

No matter what challenges we face in life, having faith in a higher power can give us the strength to carry on each day. By taking the time to focus on our spiritual needs, we can release stress and find joy in our lives. No matter what religion or beliefs you may have, honoring your faith can have a positive impact on your mental and emotional wellbeing. Spending time reading scriptures, attending services, volunteering, or simply taking a few moments each day for reflection and prayer helps us heal and grow. By embracing these practices, we can ignite a spark of renewed energy in our spiritual journey.

Many of us lead busy lives and often find it difficult to prioritize our spiritual needs. Scheduling time for yourself and making a conscious effort to nurture your relationship with the divine gets put on the back burner. By taking the time to focus on our spiritual needs, we can create powerful transformations in all aspects of our lives. We can start with small steps and gradually take more responsibility for our spiritual health.

This could be done by joining a faith-based group, participating in local events, or taking a retreat from the hustle and bustle of everyday life. Whatever it is that you choose to do, make sure your spiritual activities are meaningful and help you stay connected with what's important. With practice and dedication, you can create an environment of peace and strength within yourself. Taking time to connect with a higher power brings comfort to your faith journey and lets you live life to the fullest.

Taking time out to feed your spiritual needs can help you to stay grounded and focused on the important things in life. Honor yourself by acknowledging that you are part of something greater and knowing that peace and joy are possible. No matter what life throws at you, you can find comfort in knowing that your faith is a source of strength, and that you are connected to something greater than yourself.

Self-Reflection

When I was in third grade, I was given a bible with my name engraved on it. Ever since, this treasured possession has been like my own personal handbook to help me make sense of life's difficulties and challenges. As I grew older, I would have many conversations with the Big Guy Upstairs. I had a powerful knowing that there was a divine presence that seemed to protect and guide me. Having this awareness helped me to understand the bigger picture of life and stay grounded in reality.

For me, self-reflection involves setting aside time each day to examine my thoughts, feelings, and behaviors. I typically do this through journaling and meditation, as it allows me to process my emotions in a safe and private space.

I find that taking time throughout my day for self-reflection helps me to gain clarity about my thoughts and feelings. It allows me to gain awareness and see patterns in my behavior and identify areas where I need to make changes. One of the most healing aspects of self-reflection for me is that it allows me to take control of my own healing process. Rather than relying solely on outside sources for support, I am able to become an active participant in my own healing journey.

Throughout my life, I would often open that bible randomly to seek passages that were relevant to the situation I was dealing with. Whether it was a lesson on patience or a way to soothe my hurt feelings, I felt like God was giving me special messages to help me move forward in life. By engaging in the process of self-reflection and scripture reading, I have gained invaluable insight into my own spiritual growth. It has taught me how to make sense of the world around me and to be mindful of my thoughts and actions. My faith has become a cornerstone in my life, helping me stay connected to the divine and live with purpose. I am thankful to have a relationship with God that brings me peace and joy.

One of my favorite bible verses reads:

---

*For I know the plans I have for you, declares the Lord,
plans to prosper you and not to harm you, plans to give you
hope and a future.* ~ Jeremiah 29:11

I reflect on this verse often and find comfort in knowing that God has a plan for me, and He will never forsake me as long as I stay true to His word. This verse serves as a reminder to keep faith when going through difficult times, and it is also a source of motivation when trying to achieve my goals.

Prayer & Meditation

Have you ever felt like you were carrying the weight of the world on your shoulders? Like no matter how hard you tried, you just couldn't make things happen? Well, let me tell you, prayer is like a secret weapon to lighten that load. It's like hitting the easy button and letting God take charge of the heavy lifting. Don't get me wrong, it takes some serious humility to admit that we can't do it all on our own, but once we do, there's no limit to what God can do through us. So, grab hold of the power of prayer. Let's watch what happens when God shows up and shows out!

My mom was diagnosed with Alzheimer's disease in November of 2019. At the time, I was a mess. I was emotionally drained, physically out of shape, mentally overwhelmed and financially strapped. The only thing I had to hang my hopes on was prayer. I remember coming home, climbing into bed crying and praying.

For me, prayer is a way to communicate with God. It involves speaking from the heart, expressing gratitude, asking for guidance, and seeking comfort and support. I find that prayer can be a powerful tool for emotional healing, as it allows me to surrender my worries and fears to a higher power, and trust that everything will work out for the best.

Prayer can also be a way to seek guidance and wisdom. By asking for help in making decisions or navigating difficult situations, I am able to tap into a source of divine wisdom that can guide me towards the best course of action. This can be especially helpful when I feel stuck or unsure of what to do next. I have found that prayer is my source of comfort and support and has helped me find a greater sense of peace and well-being in my life.

Seeking Wisdom

Every time God's plan comes to light, I find myself oddly resistant, like Jonah. I question God's plan. Why me, God? Why now? Yet somehow, I just know that no matter how much resistance I put up in my head, my heart understands what needs to be done. I practice listening to my intuition and being brave enough to take the plunge into whatever new waters He may be calling me towards.

One of the most important sources of wisdom, in my healing journey, has been other people. Whether it's friends, family members, or professionals, I have found that seeking out the advice and guidance of others can be incredibly helpful. I intentionally surround myself with individuals who are positive, uplifting, and supportive. By doing so, I am able to receive a wide variety of viewpoints and the guidance necessary to navigate life's challenges.

I've learned to accept God's will and be at peace with the way he guides my life. I surrender to His plans, knowing that he has a greater purpose for me than I can even imagine. Through this journey of faith, I am constantly learning how to better seek wisdom in everything I do.

In my 20s, I heard a voice in my head nudging me to volunteer to teach Sunday School. In my 40s, that voice urged me to start a teen bible study and attend Lay Servant Ministry training. In my 50s, I began writing bible studies and contributing to multi-author collaboration books. In every instance, I sought advice and direction from mentors. It's taken many years for me to surrender and embrace the uncomfortable feeling of being outside my comfort zone and embracing my gifts. I am so thankful for this journey! It has not always been easy, but it has been filled with countless blessings, opportunities, and lessons learned along the way. I still find it hard to believe that God has chosen ME to lead and serve in different ways. My current mantra is, just say yes and figure it out on the way.

Being of Service

As I reflect back on my journey, I have discovered the power of service and how it can transform lives. There is something special about being in service to others that stirs a greater purpose within us. Through our service, we are able to offer healing to those who need it most - ourselves included. By serving others in need, we form relationships that go beyond just friendship. We become a source of hope and comfort, which helps us to build stronger connections with our faith and with one another. It is my sincere wish that each of you take the opportunity to be in service to others - whether it's in your church or in your community - and use the power of service to create positive change.

For over 30 years, I volunteered to teach Sunday School at my church. I discovered that not only was I teaching the children, but I, myself, was learning. I was reminded that service to others is an essential part of faith and builds strength in our communities. Watching the kids grow and develop a closer relationship with God was one of the most rewarding parts of my job. My experience as a teacher also made me realize how important it is to encourage young people to be actively involved in their faith.

One of the most significant benefits of volunteering is the sense of purpose and meaning it can bring to your life. When you volunteer, you are making a positive impact in the world and helping to make a difference in the lives of others. This can be incredibly rewarding and fulfilling, especially if you are struggling with your own sense of purpose or direction in life. Through volunteering, I have found a sense of purpose and fulfillment that has helped me to feel more connected to the world around me.

I have found that volunteering can be a powerful tool for personal growth and healing. By focusing on the needs of others, you can shift your focus away from your own problems and challenges. This can provide a welcome reprieve from the stresses and anxieties of daily life. Volunteering has helped me to gain a sense of perspective and to develop a greater sense of resilience and compassion.

I have seen firsthand the power of service in my own life and in the lives of others. I believe that by serving each other, we can make a difference in our communities and create a more loving world. With this belief, I am committed to helping those around me. Whether it be through mentoring, teaching, providing guidance and support, or just being a listening ear, I am here to be of service and help others heal and grow.

Attitude of Gratitude

A few years ago, I was going through a really tough time. I was a mess, and I felt like I couldn't see anything positive in my life. Then, I started practicing gratitude. I started making a conscious effort to focus on the good things in my life, no matter how small they might have seemed.

At first, it was difficult. It felt like there was nothing good to be thankful for. Then, I started to notice little things. Like the fact that I had a roof over my head and food to eat, or the smile of a stranger in the super-market. I started to write down these things in my daily planner, and I would read them back to myself when I was feeling low.

Do you want to know something cool? That attitude of gratitude helped; it gave me a little bit of light in the darkness. It helped me to see that there were still good things in my life, even if they were small. That gave me hope.

Another way to cultivate that attitude of gratitude is by focusing on the present moment. When you are mindful and fully present, you start appreciating the small things in life. The sound of birds chirping outside, the warmth of the sun on your skin, the taste of your favorite food.

For me, having an attitude of gratitude has been a powerful tool for healing. When I focus on the good things in my life, even in the midst of difficult times, it helps me to feel more positive and hopeful. Gratitude allows me to acknowledge the progress I've made in my healing journey, no matter how small it may seem. It also helps me to let go of negative emotions and to forgive those who may have hurt me. When I am grateful, I am more aware of the love and support around me, which helps me to feel less alone. Ultimately, having an attitude of gratitude has allowed me to feel more at peace and to see the world in a more positive light, which has been essential to my healing process.

Be Still and Know

One of the most powerful things I learned was the act of being still. Almost every morning, I sit quietly, set a timer, and don't move for five minutes or more. Doing this allows me to tune in to my emotions and physical sensations. When I am still, I am more aware of my body and my feelings, which helps me to identify any areas of tension or discomfort that may be holding me back in my healing journey.

Being still also helps me to slow down and gain perspective. When I am constantly on the go, it is easy to become overwhelmed and to lose sight of what is truly important. By taking the time to be still, I am able to gain a greater sense of clarity and focus, this allows me to make better decisions and to approach my healing journey with intention and purpose.

By taking intentional moments to connect with ourselves and our surroundings, we can gain greater clarity, reduce stress and anxiety, and improve our overall physical and mental health. So, take a deep breath, close your eyes, and embrace the stillness. Your mind, body, and soul will thank you.

I have come to realize that healing is not just about addressing physical symptoms, but also about nurturing our minds and spirits. By using my healing gifts to tend to my mental and emotional health, I am able to approach life with a greater sense of balance and purpose. Whether it be through stillness practices, gratitude, volunteering, or seeking wisdom from others, each step I take in my healing journey brings me closer to a more fulfilling and joyful life. As I continue to grow and heal, I hope to use my gifts to help others on their own healing paths. For in giving, we receive, and in healing ourselves, we can help to heal the world.

Let's talk about stress

Let's talk about stress and all it can do,
From ailments to headaches when I'm feeling blue,
The tears start to fall yet the anger remains,
I whine and I grumble, nag, and complain.

Too many situations that stress me each day,
Too many circumstances make me shriek in dismay,
Too many people inflaming my rage,
Too many curse words to fit on this page.

Too few occasions to sit back and relax,
Too many moments that fall through the cracks,
Too much uncertainty and not enough time,
Too many fall downs and not enough climbs.

Let's talk about prayer and all it can do,
Soothe and console, relieve and renew,
A peace starts to flow, and a happiness appears,
I pray, and I find that my stress disappears.

~Sally Larkin Green

Sally Green

Sally Green is the Vice President of Author Development at Action Takers Publishing. She works with writers to help them develop their stories and become bestselling authors. Action Takers Publishing specializes in themed, multi-author, collaboration books in which each person writes a chapter and becomes part of a community of like-minded authors. In addition to collaboration books, they also publish solo books.

At the age of 58, Sally realized that she was really good at taking care of everyone else, but really bad at taking care of herself. So, she embarked on a journey of self-care that began with investing in herself and contributing to a multi-author book. Sally is an inspirational speaker, a multiple times International Bestselling Author and is in the process of writing her own book titled, *The Self-Care Rockstar* due to launch in 2023.

In her spare time, Sally enjoys painting and teaching acrylic paint classes at local senior centers, Women's groups, and Children's summer camps.

Connect with Sally at https://www.actiontakerspublishing.com/.

CHAPTER 20

Heal Yourself So You Can Heal the World

by Shanna Lee Moore

Healing is defined as *the process of making or becoming sound or healthy again.* The definition of a gift that will apply in my chapter will be two-fold; 1) *a natural ability or talent* and 2) *a thing willingly given to another*.

My name is Shanna Lee Moore and I have been using my healing gifts consistently for the last fifteen years. My abilities and talents were noticed prior to that; however, I didn't tune in and develop them to share on a grander scale until 2006. I always had a natural ability or intuition to find the knots or trigger points in people's muscles and instinctively knew how to dissolve them to relieve pain. I remember as a child rubbing my mom's feet and ankles and working on my peers' shoulders and necks sitting behind their desks in high school. In my twenties, when I was a single mom to my oldest child, I made the decision to embrace this gift fully and went to school to become a professional massage therapist. While studying all the body systems, my mom jokingly asked why I didn't just become a nurse instead considering everything I was learning. I knew I desired more time freedom. Five- to six-hour days sounded better than twelve- to fourteen-hour days! Not only did I want to help facilitate healing in others, but my main priority was to be present and involved in my daughter's childhood. In hindsight, this was the beginning of some of my inner child healing. Now I can recognize that after doing some deeper work.

At the beginning of my massage career, I was still out of balance. I could massage, relieve pain, and help others heal, however I still felt broken. In a way, I found my worth in helping others more than myself. I didn't feel worthy of living up to my full potential. I carried around baggage in many forms; excess weight, material things in storage units, feelings of guilt, shame and regret. My internal little girl was crying out for attention. Unfortunately, I looked outside of myself for it. This led to unhealthy and sometimes toxic relationships. After surviving domestic violence, substance abuse and mental health diagnoses, my mind and body both needed healing. I didn't realize this until I started working with my first mentor/coach. She's been involved with natural wellness and a lifestyle of freedom for over four decades! I am truly grateful for Marilyn and all the wisdom she shared with me over the last ten years. This was the catalyst to the next phase of my healing journey.

Change Your Water, Change Your Life™, this short slogan has had a profound impact on my life. Water is the foundation of this planet AND our bodies! They are both approximately seventy-five percent water. Intellectually it makes perfect sense, I just hadn't given it much thought growing up. I don't really remember drinking water as a kid. In massage school, I learned about hydrating after the session to flush out toxins from the body. Now I knew I needed water, but who knew there were distinct types of water?

When I introduced electrolyzed reduced water into my body, it responded quite quickly. I lost thirty pounds in three months and was able to bring my body into homeostasis. This allowed me to discontinue using the pharmaceutical medications I was taking and start my more holistic approach to health. What we fuel our bodies with is even more important than the gas we use and the maintenance we do to our cars. We can always buy a new car; however, we only get one body. Looking back on my life choices with new awareness, I can see how I was programmed by advertisements, commercials and societal norms. Things changed in my generation drastically from the ones before. We were some of the first kids who grew up with both parents working. This made faster dinners appealing as they were tired from a full workday and not home early to prepare things from scratch. I DO remember home cooked meals and also the introduction of TV dinners and fast food. My parents split up right before my teenage years, so I'm sure having to feed myself when my mom was working made the less healthy snacks that teens like even more appealing.

To this day I still like simple things, the go to foods have just changed. An avocado or green drink smoothie is just as quick as the drive-through. I've also been blessed with an amazing chef for a husband. Food adjustments can be a little more challenging to address since eating often involves emotions and socializing. I didn't learn about reading labels for ingredients until I showed up at a potluck one day with store bought potato salad. What a revelation that was! As a general practice for beginners I'll share this: if I can't pronounce it or don't know what it is, I probably don't want to consume it. There will always be a few exceptions since I follow the 80/20 rule. I leave that little bit of wiggle room to explore new experiences or old things that I enjoyed growing up.

What I can tell you is that by tuning in to my body it will let me know whether or not something is in harmony. It may respond with a physical symptom such as a headache or feelings of fatigue, and sometimes it's a vibrational or energetic feeling. That gut instinct we have is part of our nervous system. Since a great deal of my life was spent in trauma responses, it's been a new experience for me to go within and heal myself and tune in to the higher faculties. I am still a work in progress and have by no means ARRIVED at my destination.

Even this week writing this chapter, I experienced feelings of overwhelm and had a few breakdowns. That is something that before I may have tried to run away from. Introspection allows me to have more clarity and my toolbox is much bigger now. So often it's not the EVENT that has happened that impacts us, as it is the story about it we retell over and over to ourselves. This is just one more awareness and discovery I've had. Keeping in mind, we are social creatures and benefit from healthy relationships, not all of these thoughts came solely from me. This brings me back to the programming I mentioned before. If we go through life unaware of what information we feed our minds, we will be living a life of DEFAULT, not DESIGN. We are bombarded with between 4,000 and 10,000 ads daily, so it's important to be intentional with what we read, watch, listen to and who we associate with. I notice I pick up traits and habits from those around me. We really do become like the people we spend time with. Just last week, I heard a song lyric that reminded me of a line from a movie that I saw when I was fifteen years old. That quote has completely influenced one of my guiding paradigms that I have still been living by as an adult. The brain is fascinating.

I've heard it said by Dr. Greg S. Reid that, "What is common sense for one person can be genius for another." One story I have that comes to mind was when my dear friend Margot had chicken that needed to be cooked. She was called out for an urgent matter and was worried it would go bad since she didn't have time to prepare it. The first thing that came to my mind was to use the crock pot. She said she would have never thought of it.

Collaborating and sharing ideas with positive, uplifting people is part of why I'm so dedicated to building communities. When I am in the presence of others working to improve themselves and their situations, together we can create great things. We are all just one person, idea, decision or innovation away from a totally different life. I found there are far more people willing to encourage, support and help you than there are who want to put you down.

My life wasn't always that way though. First, I had to decide what I wanted. Did I want to grumble and be unhappy or did I want to heal myself and share hope with others? Did I want to stay stuck in old unhealthy routines and habits or did I want to open my mind and expand? After the DECISION is made, all of the future circumstances will either contribute or distract from that goal. My decision is to live a life I love, in my true nature and purpose. I am a healer, a helper, a connector, and an inspiration. I am a woman, a daughter, a mother, a wife and a friend. I will challenge you lovingly to think outside the Box. I will teach you how to get what you want as long as you're willing to be open to new possibilities. I will continue to grow myself and not get stuck in stagnation or complacency. The world is a stage and life is our movie. Just remember to cast yourself as the shining star in yours, not just a supporting character.

This has probably been the most challenging chapter I've written. So many stalls, hiccups and transitions have happened since I started. I share this to display the humanness inside me and in us all. Also, to give encouragement to you that you don't have to let perfectionism or procrastination hinder you from sharing your gifts with the world. I believe we are all connected and we came here to be in community with each other. There are many religious, spiritual, philosophical and metaphysical scriptures, practices, beliefs and quotes by great beings to support this. Even the science behind us needing love and physical affection as infants to survive. I don't believe this goes away as we age into adulthood. Unfortunately, some don't choose to use the experiences of life to learn lessons and instead build up walls.

That was me for a long time. I was numb. I didn't know who I was or how I got so far from the person I wanted to be. I lost myself in my relationships, taking care of others' needs before my own. In being BUSY and not productive, not effectively prioritizing the things that will truly get me to my goals. Shutting down from overwhelm or zoning out with distractions. I had to break the cycle. How do I need to be and carry myself NOW to support all the growth I expect to have? What is it that I truly want and won't settle for any less than?

I used to be so bothered by the phrase *fake it 'til you make it*. I never wanted to be FAKE. What I realize now is that when I play small and stay in my comfort zone, I'm not living in my truth and sharing vulnerabilities. Now I'll say, *faith it 'til you make it*. There is a great power working behind our thoughts and words. When we dare to dream, really dream, with clarity and conviction that is what creates the changes. Having the faith to believe in the abundance this world has to offer. Having the courage to go against the norm and swim upstream. Having the insight to evaluate yourself and pivot along the way. As long as I breathe deep and stay present in the moment I have nothing to fear. Most of my issues arise when I'm thinking about the past or the future. Of course, this takes mindfulness and practice and is easier said than done.

This brings us back around to our support system. This year, my community has grown. I have learned more about myself and spent a lot of time in self-reflection on old beliefs and patterns. The inner clarity and understanding of what my needs are has helped me to be able to express my boundaries and desires in a way that I wasn't able to in the past. Is it still challenging at times? Of course! For me especially, the boundaries part. As a recovering people pleaser, it is hard to put my needs first. Somewhere, I learned or picked up the notion that if I didn't help someone or if I took care of myself first that I was cold hearted or selfish. My natural instinct is still to offer help when I can. Now, I just make sure that it's not going to be at the expense of myself. Part of this healing has come from working with others who have journeyed this path before me. With all the new things I start to do, I find someone who's done it before to glean wisdom from.

We can find this wisdom in various places like books, podcasts, YouTube videos, Ted talks, and courses. Also, from being in association with like-minded or even better, elevated minded individuals. I know sometimes I'm not able to pull myself up on my own, so being with others who've reached a higher place is an inspiration. My internal healing came when I finally understood that I could use others' stories to find commonality and empathy while still being true to myself and honoring my own experiences. Just because someone has had a different situation happen doesn't make one right and the other wrong. Showing up as an observer and leaving room for others to process and be in their own feelings and emotions has given me insight on my own. We were created as unique creatures and we ALL have special gifts and talents to offer the world.

What's most alive in me today? Continuing to grow into the best version of myself while assisting others in achieving their full potential. We are capable of so much more than we give ourselves credit for! We all deserve to live the life of our dreams. I love connecting with people who want to make a difference in the world. Those who know they have something special inside them. Maybe they just need to be reminded from time to time. When the weight of the world feels too heavy, it's our friends and associates who can help ease the burden. Just be mindful that those you surround yourself with will help carry the load and not throw more weight on. Maybe you aren't sure what gifts you have or what lights you up? I would love to brainstorm with you as well. All we need is that little loving push and perspective. So if you've been confused, lost or looking for more, please reach out. I'd love to welcome you into my tribe with open arms and a big hug!

Healing myself so I can help heal the world,

It seemed like an overwhelming task.

I had to go within and under all of my shadows,

Before I could come out in the sun and bask.

Some trauma was deep,

Some cords were strong.

Some of it was easier to clear,

And some took very long.

I keep showing up and moving forward,

To be an example to all I meet.

I will not stop until I have succeeded,

I will not settle for defeat!

I have the love from within and up above,

Shining down on me.

Finding my tribe and community,

Now I can really be free.

Free to grow and heal the past,

Free to travel to the highest mountain.

Nurturing my body and soul daily,

Drinking from the purest fountain.

I once was lost and scared,

Also, timid and shy.

Questioning my purpose here,

Not knowing exactly why…

Why did things unfold as they did?

What was the lesson for me to learn?

You may have asked these questions too,

So now it is your turn.

To go within and seek your truth,

To find your answers here.

Then reach out to those like you,

There is no reason to fear.

We all come with love happy to help,

There is no judgment from us.

We welcome you with open arms,

Your presence is a plus!

You are loved and wanted here,

We have been waiting for you to arrive.

Now is time to relax in the flow,

No longer pushing to strive.

All that is for you will surely come,

It's already on its way.

Just breathe deep and stay in the moment,

It's all about today!

Shanna Lee Moore

Shanna Lee Moore is an entrepreneur, business owner, and award winning, #1 international bestselling author. Shanna has been a member of the National Certification Board for Therapeutic Massage and Bodywork and practicing as a Licensed Massage Therapist since 2007 in San Diego, California. After personally having profound health changes, she started sharing the benefits of electrolyzed, reduced water with her clients and the world in 2012.

After the 2020 shutdown, Shanna focused more on building her community and started speaking at virtual events. Shanna was able to use self-reflection and insight and she has grown in new ways. She's learned to love herself and has started attracting those who resonate with her authenticity and vulnerability.

One of the things she loves most is helping others create the life they've always wanted. Shanna offers creative solutions and out-of-the-box thinking to help people balance their families and businesses. If you aren't sure what gifts you have or what lights you up, Shanna would love to brainstorm with you. She loves connecting with motivated, passionate people both in person and virtually.

Connect with Shanna at

https://calendly.com/shannaleemoore/30min.

CHAPTER 21

From Grief to Grace

by Tiffiny Jewel Roper

I had to find a way to move on, to heal, after losing my twins, Braden and Karissa, at twenty weeks pregnant. An "incompetent cervix" issue had forced my body into early labor with otherwise healthy, growing babies. The grief was overwhelming, and I didn't know how to move on. I struggled with where to start healing. Every day, anytime I was alone or falling asleep, I had constant flashes of memory of this horrific loss spinning through my head, on automatic repeat. I mean, how can the world go on without my beautiful babies? How could I? Where do you start when you don't know how to make it through an hour or a day...when you can't stop crying?

I held my sweet babies, alive, in my arms for three and four hours, not able to do anything to help them. The feeling was horrendous, such despair. I watched them struggle, and slowly die, not being able to breathe on their own because their lungs weren't fully developed. I held them as their heartbeats finally stopped. I was their Mommy, and I was supposed to protect them and keep them safe. After so many years of struggling to get pregnant, I had already felt like I wasn't "woman" enough to get pregnant without help. We conceived these babies through IVF (in-vitro fertilization). I knew women that had had miscarriages when there was something wrong with the baby, but I'd never heard of anyone losing perfectly healthy babies (outside of abortion). I, as their Mommy, had failed them.

When I was at the hospital, after birth, I lost so much blood that I had to have a blood transfusion. I asked the doctor what would happen if I didn't have the transfusion, and she said I would go home and probably have a heart attack and possibly die. I remember thinking, "that sounds good, then I can be with my babies again." I didn't want to go on, to continue living without them. I decided to get a blood transfusion, for my family, despite my feelings. Later that day, the day of my babies' birth and ultimate death, the nurse brought in my babies, covered in a small white blanket, and said, "take as long as you need to say goodbye to them." I immediately thought to myself, "how much time is enough?" How do you say goodbye to these sweet, super tiny, yet perfectly formed and beautiful babies? To my surprise, they even had fingernails, eyebrows, and eyelashes. I remember sitting with them, holding them, talking to them, apologizing to them for not keeping them safe, for having failed them. I told them how much I loved them and always would. I cried over them, watching my tears fall onto the blankets covering them.

Going home with empty arms to a house that was being prepared for babies, with a book the hospital gave me called, *"Empty Arms,"* in case I had forgotten, was heartbreaking. I wondered why the world was still spinning around, and I was mad. How dare the world go on when my babies were no longer a part of it? I kept reliving the experience and feeling of giving birth, of the babies leaving my body, watching them slowly die as I held them. A few days later, we had the funeral. I didn't know how to do that either. How do I say my final goodbye? The funeral itself while dealing with the emotions of others hurting at the funeral, was very difficult. Standing by my babies' tiny casket with my husband, reading a poem I wrote for them, watching everyone's tears fall around me, knowing this was really goodbye, was too much.

After the funeral, people went back to their regular lives and expected me to go back to mine. However, I didn't know how to go on. My whole world had been flipped upside-down and I was truly in pain and suffering. There was no more "normal." I rarely heard from anyone after that; people felt like they had "done their job" by going to the funeral, while I was struggling all day. My head was often filled with the horrible memories, over and over, on a never-ending cycle. My heart felt so very heavy. It felt like an elephant was sitting on top of it. I didn't know how to stop hurting so much. One night, I was so overwhelmed with the grief and pain I laid in bed and begged God to take some of my pain, to help me hold it because I wasn't strong enough to take it all on myself. Thankfully, the next morning, I did feel lighter. I was still in so much pain, but it was the first day I felt like I could finally start my healing journey.

For a couple of weeks after my babies passed, my husband was amazing and sat with me for hours as I cried, and he held my hand. Then, after about two weeks, I could tell he was ready to move on, or maybe he decided to tuck away his pain to keep going in his own way. I saw him play video games a lot more, and I knew that if I kept going to him with my pain, I would be bringing him down and keeping him from moving on, and it made me feel guilty. Thankfully, I had my amazing Dad, who was willing to talk to me for hours into the night, despite his own health issues, anytime I needed to talk to someone or I needed to cry. At one point, I went to a therapist, just trying to figure out how to survive after that first week of loss, and all she could tell me was "just cry." That was her answer? Nothing against therapy, but I could tell she hadn't been through it, and she truly didn't understand or empathize with my pain. At the end of the session, I felt worse. I never went back to her. Then, I found an infant loss support group where there were other couples that were struggling with a similar loss. My husband didn't want to attend the classes, so my dad offered to go with me, so I wasn't alone. I never asked him, and I thought I would be okay going by myself, but he truly knew me better than I knew myself. He was there for me when I desperately needed it.

Attending the support group, even though we all had lost our babies in different ways, it was helpful to talk about my loss and know I wasn't alone. I also found an internet group for women that had lost babies because of an incompetent cervix. It was the most helpful thing, talking with other women who had lost babies in the same way and reason I had. I knew they understood. Later, I reached out to women who had just gone through their loss to help them, like others were helping me. I met some amazing, strong women in that group and attribute it, and my dad's unwavering support, to why I have my sanity today.

I learned a lot of lessons during this time of my life. I learned to take it one hour at a time, then one day at a time. I learned to find support, so I didn't feel alone. I learned to reach out to others and support them, so I could get out of my own pain for a second (though I was also living through it again while I helped them get through their loss). Often, I've found, the way to heal ourselves when we are suffering, is to help others who are also suffering. In addition, I found that I had to create boundaries with some people who said painful things to me. While they thought it was helpful, it wasn't. When someone loses a child, through miscarriage or otherwise, statements, such as "well, they are in a better place" (better than mommy's arms?), or "you can always have another child" (so if you lose your spouse or an adult child, should I say the same?), are very hurtful. So many people don't know what to say, so they just stay away, which makes the person grieving feel even more alone.

So, what's the best way to handle it? If someone is grieving, there are often no words that will make them feel better, so know it is fine to just say nothing. Or you can say, "I know there are no words to make this better, but I want to just be here for you," then sit with them and hold their hand and shoulder some of the pain, so they don't have to bear the weight of it all on their own. Also, I learned that men and women grieve losing a child in different ways and timeframes. It is estimated that eighty percent of marriages will divorce or separate after losing a child. My belief is that it's partially because they aren't giving each other the grace or understanding that we grieve differently. For an early loss, as the one I had, the women have held these babies for several months before the loss and are suffering in a different way because of that longer connection. Also, females are generally more in touch with their emotions than males, so they have to go through loss differently. In that same vain, since men and women grieve differently, women need to not judge men for how they grieve. Because we don't see them showing "enough emotion" doesn't mean they aren't grieving. Grace and kindness, not blame and shame, is the way forward, if you want your relationship to survive such a loss.

After a needed surgery and a few months, we were pregnant again with amazing twin girls. While some wondered if I was moving too fast, I knew myself well enough to know I needed this to help me move on. However, after such a traumatic loss, I was terrified. Every day was scary. I struggled getting through the first trimester, often the most dangerous one, but knew I still wasn't safe. Previously, my loss was in the second trimester. This time, I had to know I was going to get through it. The big mark to hit this time in my pregnancy was twenty-eight weeks. On that day, I was truly elated. I knew if my babies were born then, they would most likely survive. My dad was so happy for me, even though, just days before he had fallen and broken his rib and was in a good amount of pain.

On day twenty-eight and one day, out of nowhere, my dad passed away. He was my heart, my strength, everything to me. I was, and always will be, "Daddy's girl." He saved my sanity through the loss of my babies. He was there for the worst day of my life, and I felt I owed him the best day of my life: the day when my girls were born. My pain was immeasurable. How do I say goodbye to the man that made me who I am, the man that role modeled what a loving, giving, father looked like, and someone to look to when raising my own daughters. Now he was gone, unexpectedly. In less than a year, I was planning another funeral, and I was in utter shock.

A couple of months later, I was having my beautiful babies, Avery and Sophia, at thirty-eight weeks, the standard time they deliver twins. Meeting my girls was the best day of my life and truly felt like a dream. A dream that I thought, for many years, would never come true. I remember looking in my babies' eyes and seeing how deep their souls were and immediately knew love like I had never known before, the same love my dad had for me. In losing my dad, I had to learn his love didn't go anywhere, it was just in a new form. It was a form of energy I needed to get to know and feel in a new way. Now, I see my dad in every yellow butterfly that passes by me, in front of me, leading the way when I am on a path or driving, always watching out for me and my girls. I asked my dad, after losing my babies, if he would take care of them in Heaven, until I got there. These days, I know my dad is in Heaven, enjoying being a Papa to my babies and loving them and playing with them.

When my girls were two days old, I started feeling like I couldn't breathe when I laid back to breastfeed. I had panic attacks after losing my babies, and my sister thought I may be going through another one. They did x-rays on me, and days before Christmas, I learned I had cardiomyopathy, heart failure caused by my pregnancy. One-in-fifteen thousand pregnant women have this, after my one-in-one hundred diagnosis of incompetent cervix, and I couldn't believe it. My girls were taken away from me in the hospital, and I was moved to a different room and put on oxygen for twenty-four hours. After my diagnosis, I was told I needed lots of sleep and couldn't have any stress. I laughed, through my fear, telling them I'd just had twins, so wish me luck. My precious girls liked to take turns getting up every two hours. That allowed me to take care of one of them at a time, but that also meant I only got about thirty minutes of sleep a night. At that time, they also told me I'd need a heart transplant within five years, and the average lifespan of a heart or lung transplant patient was about five years, so I may not live long enough for my girls to turn ten. I was, again, in utter shock. My family helped me with my girls as much as they could. One sister had her teen daughter stay the night to help for a few weeks. My other sister took the babies overnight a couple of times with her girls. My mom came a few times and watched the babies, while she barely slept, so I could get a little rest.

After getting used to the medications they gave me, and working up to exercise again, and slowly getting my ejection fraction back to a more tolerable range over the years, I started feeling like there was some hope for a longer life. I am grateful and proud to say my amazing daughters just turned ten a few months ago, and I am still here, without a heart transplant.

Through all of the pain I've been through, I had to find a reason why I was going through it. For many years, I couldn't understand why I had gone through so much. I just had to trust, one day, it would make sense, so I could move on. When I really started focusing on my personal development, I started realizing why I had gone through the pain I had gone through. Though I'd always been a very empathetic person, going through the grief I had, feeling like I had no interest in continuing my life, and having to get through that to where I am now, I realized it was going to make me a much better person and Life Coach. The thing missing from the therapist I went to, after losing the babies, was the fact that she hadn't been through something similar. She really didn't get it, and I could feel that. With everything I've been through, I have no doubt I can help the Moms I coach get results. With that, and the twenty years of project management experience under my belt, I know how to keep clients accountable to stay on track, and I believe in them and their new possibilities, until they believe in themselves as well.

I've also learned the power of feminine energy: creativeness, intuition, resourcefulness, divine power, nurturing, loving, and giving. Being raised by such a strong, masculine man, in a generation of women that were raised to not ever "depend on a man," I saw myself being in my masculine more than my feminine. I had issues with female family members and friends that caused me to not trust the feminine, and I never truly understood the true power of the feminine energy. Once I had my girls, I never felt more feminine. I also learned to love my body, instead of blaming it for failing me and my babies. After all, it grew these amazing beings I have now. I started stepping into my feminine energy more, and I truly felt like myself, without the masculine mask I'd been wearing in a masculine IT corporate world for twenty years. If you are like me, and you don't have enough positive, amazing, female role models around you, then make friends that love you, and raise you up, and want your happiness as much as they want their own. Unfortunately, there aren't enough women that do this for each other because they have often been conditioned to see each other as competition instead of realizing there is enough for everyone. The more women succeed, the more women will succeed.

I've been through a long journey, but I wouldn't change anything. Despite the pain, I am who I am, the mom and the Life Coach, because of what I have been through. I hope I can inspire others to find their own joy and fulfillment and know they, too, can make it through anything and can, themselves, find the grace needed to get through it all, as I have successfully gone from grief to grace.

Tiffiny Roper

Tiffiny Roper is on a mission to create amazing female leaders of tomorrow that this world desperately needs. She accomplishes this as a Life Coach for Moms of young daughters, working passionately with them to reach their goals and becoming the best role models they can be. In doing so, they live with a new purpose-driven life filled with joy and inspire those around them to do the same, starting with their daughters. She uses her twenty years of Project Management experience to keep Moms accountable in hitting their goals. She's also a speaker and best-selling author that loves creating memories with her husband of twenty years and young twin daughters, Avery and Sophia, including coaching their softball team and leading their Girl Scout troop.

Connect with Tiffiny at

https://www.facebook.com/groups/girlmomcoaching.

CHAPTER 22

———— ❧ ————

Rise... and Walk

by Victoria Rader

Healing is not an event, it is a process that sustains life, all of life, all the time. ~Victoria Rader

---

The strength of emotion was overwhelming and beyond my mental capacity to express it through language. Every cell of my body felt. I felt... fully alive. I felt the presence of miracles at this site of many miracles, where I stood by the ruins of the pool of Bethesda.

Over two thousand years ago the pure healing waters of the pool of Bethesda summoned the sick, the lame, and the blind with the sacred powers of restoring wholeness. Those that would reach the waters right after the angels moved the waters were healed. Whereas others would spend time waiting for their turn to experience a miracle. It was also here by the pools of Bethesda that Jesus healed a man who was too weak to reach the waters. With the divine power of commanding the elements, the Savior invited the man to *rise... and walk.* (John 5:8)

One of my favorite paintings is of Christ healing at the pool of Bethesda. I have it in my home and in my studio. I carry it with me in my heart; and it is my heart that was experiencing all the power of the emotion of life, offering love of God, inviting me to *rise... and walk.*

I could feel the powerful healing call to *rise... and walk* in every cell of my body: to rise above each daily trial and to walk my path. I savored the moment. Miraculous healings, resolving both in life and in death, have flooded my heart with a renewed understanding that healing was not a moment. It was not an event. Healing is a process that sustains life, all of life, all the time. Which is why a loss experienced with transition of any form of life invites us to open and to heal.

For me, miscarrying a life was one of the first profound invitations to heal. When you expect a baby, you expect to see life expand through you in the most unique way. A tiny part of you is carried on creating a new physical expression of divine love. When you miscarry, you experience loss of a physical life to be, and also a spiritual expectation of that life, and a literal part of you.

I was unaware of what was happening to my body, feeling feverish and sitting at the baseball game. I was with my husband and his friends far away from home. This was my first pregnancy and it was ending. I was in complete shock. With time, the shock gave way to healing. I could not verbalize or explain it, but there was a deep knowing and an even deeper comfort. I allowed myself to receive the healing. As people, we cannot force healing; we can only accept it when it is offered through experiencing God's grace.

A year later, I held my daughter Lydia in my arms. Holding my baby girl has redefined my perception of reality and meaning of life. Life is the meaning of life: supporting life, sustaining life, nourishing life, all through surrendering to LOVE, Life-Originating Vibrant Emotion (Energy-in-motion). LOVE creates all life. I felt overwhelming joy in witnessing a miracle of life unfold. I was coming to terms with my own inadequacy as a mother. Hormonal, sad, and challenged, yet seeking and finding peace. Over and over again, feeling the call to *rise... and walk.* I would pray for strength to walk and for guidance to help others through this mortal experience of healing that we refer to as life.

One evening, I was visiting a dear friend from my church. She was going through a challenging time, and I earnestly prayed to know how to best support her. I shared with her Isaiah 53, describing Messiah, *He is despised and rejected of men; a man of sorrows, and acquainted with grief... surely he has born our griefs, and carried our sorrows... he was wounded... he was bruised... the chastisement of our peace was upon him; and with his stripes we are healed.* She saw herself in those words, a woman of sorrow, acquainted with grief, now present in the space created by the words of the ancient prophet. She allowed for the depth of the healing to come into her heart, surpassing her understanding. While it did not shift the circumstances of her life, it did shift her perception. She answered the call to *rise... and walk* as an empowered divine daughter of God. The transformation mesmerized me.

It was on that same day, in the evening, I was miscarrying yet another life, at the end of my first trimester. In pain and grieving, I was also humbled by the deep realization that the scripture I shared with my friend, was shared by the Spirit not only by me and through me, but also for me. There were physical complications and more grief that followed. Yet, amidst all of the turmoil, I quietly discerned a beautiful whisper of peaceful hope through healing. *Rise... and walk.*

My baby boy, Ray, came into my life after that heartrending miscarriage. He was such a quiet baby that I would stand over his crib to hear him breathing. He was ok. I was not. I was afraid of losing him or my daughter. The loss of life caused fear of loss of life. When we set expectations of what healing is, we can become uncomfortable with wholeness. There is a part of us that doesn't know how to heal without going through suffering. The scared part of us, which I call *scared me*, is always in need of healing. Fear shows up in different ways and forms as our inability to accept the complete lack of control over external circumstances and outcomes. Healing invites us to lean into the quietness within, to find and connect to our *Sacred mE*, the LOVE that we are. Healing calls for life to unfold without forcing it, but trusting divine power to unfold through it.

It is a delicate balance to hear an invitation to heal and to pursue it despite any doubt or limitations offered by those around you. Such was an experience with my sweet girl, who was just around four years old and woke in the middle of the night complaining of the sharp pain in her abdomen. We had already experienced the challenges of stomach flu and various bugs, but this felt different. How is that for a medical diagnosis? My husband gave Lydia a priesthood blessing, which is a special ordinance to call upon God to ask for healing. Randy is an eloquent speaker and is very selective and impactful with his words. When I heard him say something along the lines of, "*and let this disease be taken out of her body,*" something in me shifted and tensed.

Even though she slept very well, she was still in pain when she woke up. I discerned a quiet message inside my mind, a whisper from the Spirit, *she has appendicitis... take her to the doctor.* Prior to the powers of the all-knowing Google, I was only equipped with a book on diagnosing diseases in children, I followed the book's suggestion to gently press on her belly button. The premise of this exercise was to observe the level of pain. If the pain was more during applying the pressure, it was likely to be flu or indigestion. If the pain was more when releasing the pressure, it was likely to be appendicitis. My little girl, with her eyes full of tears, confirmed that it hurt more after I released my hand. I packed a ton of library books, and drove to the doctor's office.

Our long day had just begun. In a gently comforting voice, the nurse practitioner informed us they were sending us home. In the practice of several doctors, I insisted on a second opinion. Then, yet, a third. The third doctor, who was quite a bit older, examined Lydia and stated that even though he had never seen appendicitis in a child this young, if I felt this immense urgency, to take her to the emergency room. Hours of waiting proceeded with us being brushed aside, and put behind every new patient arriving. They were deemed to be in a more urgent state. Toward the end of the day, my husband Randy joined us, finally being able to leave work. He brought my mom so I could nurse Ray while staying at the hospital with Lydia.

Randy insisted that Lydia have an MRI. We had to sign a disclaimer that if the MRI for Lydia showed negative results that we would have to pay for it out of pocket. This was because the hospital advised against an MRI seeing it as a frivolous demand. I do not remember the amount quoted, only the suffocating feeling of not being able to afford it. Yet, we persisted.

When they brought Lydia back from radiology, the energy was quite different. The nurses and the staff were immediately apologetic. She had severe appendicitis and was scheduled for surgery that day. Due to the circumstances, we were given an incredible doctor, who performed a skillful procedure laparoscopically, allowing my little girl to be playing within days.

I will never forget Lydia's huge gorgeous green bluish eyes throughout the day. She handled the day better than any of the adults.

Even through fear of the unknown, there was a depth of trust in those eyes that gave me immense strength to persevere. I have thought of that day so many times throughout my life. Some of the trials of leaning into the guidance of the still small voice were much longer than a day. Healing my shyness took months, while healing my broken heart from some devastating betrayals and losses took years. Months and years, one day at a time, leaning into the simplicity of invitation to heal, *rise... and walk.*

We do not heal in order to be healed. We heal to be alive. Every day is an invitation to heal. Yes, there are healing modalities that I continually master, but life itself is a continual healing. Every second millions of your cells shift as some die and some are born. So, too, are the thoughts and the emotions. There isn't a status quo of bliss. There is a beautiful process of continual healing. Accepting this process fully and completely is what brings a feeling of bliss.

One of the greatest healings we can go through is accepting death as a part of life and as a process of healing. Accepting death fully allows us to also accept life fully, which gives meaning, gratitude, and appreciation to every breath we take. Our mortal life begins with a breath and ends with a breath. Breathing is life to the physical body. Thus, breathing is healing.

Hypopressive breathing is one of the most amazing ways to heal your body! *Breathe mE: Hypopressive Breathing with Nanda* is the first program of this kind in the US, because Nanda (Fernanda Semenyuk) is the first hypopressive breathing coach in the US! It is an incredible healing gift.

Nanda is my sister-in-law, and one of the most talented people I know. She plays guitar and has a gorgeous voice. She is an inspired artist. One of my favorite paintings in my office studio is a gift from her. It is an image of hands stretched up through the brilliant colors of the rainbow. This painting has a healing message from God to me continually expanding my understanding. The message has a true power within it because it was painted through LOVE. LOVE makes all things grow. Nanda pours LOVE into everything she does. As a result, anything Nanda puts her mind to and her heart into blossoms. *The Breathe mE* program is no exception.

In the title of *Breathe mE,* the little 'm' of our mortal matter surrenders through LOVE to the big 'E' of our Eternal Energy. Physical life happens as Energy moves through matter with every breath. Our lungs are a physical organ of birthing breath. We process our deepest grief and our greatest joy through our lungs, and through the patterns of our breath. Grief carves the pathways within our very soul for the joy to flow through and to heal. Healing is not avoiding grief. It is accepting it so fully that God's LOVE can reach into the very depth of our wounded soul.

Nanda's *Breathe mE* program awakens power, life, and joy because Nanda is no stranger to grief. One of the most devastating losses I have witnessed her go through and grow through was that of her precious niece.

Little Brenda fell into the pool and almost drowned. For months, the doctors in Brazil fought for her life. For months we prayed, sent healing, and hoped for a miracle. God did not grant us the miracle that we wanted, but a greater miracle of peace and realization of the importance of every breath of life. Brenda's death has given meaning to life for all of those left behind.

I have faithfully leaned into and practiced all of my healing gifts. After all, in my practice, I have witnessed so many physical, mental miracles, and recoveries through God's grace. I prayed. I did distant quantum healing. Through ThetaHealing® meditation, I witnessed processes that were later confirmed by doctors. Over time, Brenda seemed to be getting better in reclaiming some of her brain activity. There was no question that the body was healing. Yet, her powerful little spirit has finished its journey on this planet. and chose to exit as a part of her healing journey. She slipped away into a new realm of life. Life is, it continues. Life changes form. Life expands. The more aware we become of life's expansion the more alive we feel as we surrender to the healing process of restoring our wholeness.

While lingering on this planet, Brenda had become one of the greatest little teachers. She taught so many how to hope, how to persevere, how to find peace, and how to make life matter. One of the greatest lessons I have learned through the process was the power of each and every individual healing intention. Everyone prayed and sent healing to Brenda on a set day and time. After praying, I started to meditate and was shown a beautiful vision. I saw infinite sparks of light flying through the cosmos creating a blueprint in space. I have asked God to explain to me what I was witnessing. I was told that every time any of us adds a thought of love, a prayer, an intention, or a healing meditation to someone else, there is a blueprint of hope that is being added to a higher spiritual reality of creation. If that blueprint is aligned with the person's divine timing, it unfolds into the physical reality once the spiritual creation is complete. If it is not aligned, a better, brighter, and more radiant reality unfolds in response to our efforts. All the while, the spiritual invitation to *rise... and walk* asserts itself.

If you are reading this chapter at this moment in your life, it is simply a reminder of how deeply loved you are by your Creator, and of your immense ability to heal. You do not need to master or force this power, you are simply invited to surrender to God's LOVE. God's grace is here for you, moving through you. No matter what you are going through, do not give up!

When you feel like giving up, give it up instead. Whatever it is that is burdening you. Give it up to God. When you cannot continue, trust God to carry you through. Never ever give up… Give it up. Then *rise… and walk.*

Victoria Rader, Ph.D.

Victoria Rader, Ph.D. Possibility Coach™, transformational speaker, founder of YU2SHINE, internationally best-selling author, creator of Empower-mE and Master-mE apps, founder of Free mE EFT and Quantum Freedom.

Victoria empowers her clients to grow and heal in all areas of their life through the proven formula of success so that they have more PEACE, PURPOSE, and PROSPERITY.

In 2009, during the recession, Victoria became a successful top one percent of real estate agents while homeschooling her kids. Victoria started training and seeing the limitations imposed by the subconscious mind. Later she received a PhD in Metaphysics to understand better how we create our daily reality. Victoria also got certified in many energy healing modalities and traditional success coaching approaches and have founded Free mE EFT and Quantum Freedom techniques as a way to free one's mind.

In her practice, Victoria witnessed physical healings for her clients, including a miraculous heart healing for her nephew; as well as practical powerful shifts in finances, career, and relationships.

Victoria loves teaching on the universal/God's laws and their practical daily application for people of faith and spiritual seekers – bridging the gap of judgment through LOVE (Life-Originating Vibrant Emotion).

Connect with Victoria at www.ManifestMiracles.mE.

READER BONUS!

Dear Reader,

As a thank you for your support, Action Takers Publishing would like to offer you a special reader bonus: a free download of our course, "How to Write, Publish, Market & Monetize Your Book the Fast, Fun & Easy Way." This comprehensive course is designed to provide you with the tools and knowledge you need to bring your book to life and turn it into a successful venture.

The course typically **retails for $499**, but as a valued reader, you can access it for free. To claim your free download, simply follow this link ActionTakersPublishing.com/workshops - use the discount code "coursefree" to get a 100% discount and start writing your book today.

If we are still giving away this course by the time you're reading this book, head straight over to your computer and start the course now. It's absolutely free.

READER BONUS!

ActionTakersPublishing.com/workshops
discount code "coursefree"

www.ingramcontent.com/pod-product-compliance
Lightning Source LLC
Chambersburg PA
CBHW061143120626
46546CB00005B/1908